Capture
The
Courage

A Study of Acts 1-12

Be Courageous!

Scott Gleaves

8-1-04

Capture *The* Courage

A Study of Acts 1-12

G. Scott Gleaves

Gospel Advocate Company
Nashville, Tennessee

Published by Gospel Advocate Co.
1006 Elm Hill Pike, Nashville, TN 37202
http://www.gospeladvocate.com

ISBN: 0-89225-537-4

Acknowledgements

I want to express my gratitude to Jerry Callens, Jack Lynch, Pat Hogan, Bob Milligan, Dr. Thomas H. Holland and the late Robert D. Bankes for reading all or parts of my manuscript. Their suggestions and comments were extremely helpful and insightful.

I also want to express my gratitude to my spiritual brothers and sisters at the Timberlane Church of Christ in Tallahassee, Fla., for their love, encouragement and demand for relevant, biblical preaching.

I must give a special word of thanks to the late Dr. F. Furman Kearley for writing the foreword to this book. He was and continues to be a true giant in the faith and a mentor to many of us who preach and teach.

My wife, Sherri, and my children, Lindsay, Nathan and Taylor, provide my daily dose of inspiration.

I want to dedicate this book to my daddy, Jerrell Gleaves. Because of his efforts and influence, I became a Christian and a member of the Lord's most glorious church.

Table of Contents

Foreword

Teachers and preachers are constantly challenged to make vital, critical and essential material fresh and interesting to students. Those of us who are of strong faith and deeply committed to God and Christ know that the Bible is truly the most interesting and fascinating book ever written. We find fresh delight every time we open its pages.

Tragically, however, most people in our world do not know this pleasure. They are unfamiliar with the Bible, and many view it as an old, out-of-date and out-of-touch book. The great challenge of preachers and teachers is to reach those who do not know the Bible and are often repelled by its unfamiliar characters, places and events and by its commands and demands on the lives of its readers.

Brother G. Scott Gleaves has made a significant and beneficial contribution to preachers, teachers and Bible readers in his excellent book, *Capture the Courage*. This book is a unique and highly interesting presentation of the powerful message of Acts chapters 1 through 12. By the use of contemporary illustrations, Brother Gleaves makes the characters and events of Acts come alive. His presentation is unique, interesting and challenging. The fearlessness, courage and boldness of the early Christians, and their deep faith and commitment, are made real by comparison to contemporary people and events. As one reads anew the accounts of the early Christians, he is made to feel that he is there and knows them personally and is experiencing them. Brother Gleaves' account inspires, encourages and assists us to imitate the dedication and boldness of the early Christians.

I believe each reader will be thrilled as he studies Acts aided by the insights of Brother Gleaves. Those who already know Acts well will experience a freshness and reinvigoration as they explore this material.

Dr. F. Furman Kearley
Former Senior Editor
Gospel Advocate
2003

Introduction

The book of Acts is the most exciting book in the New Testament. At one time the book of Acts was the training manual of the church. People were converted to Christ by appealing to its examples of conversion. The church maintained her identity by appealing to its examples of Christian behavior. New Christians were indoctrinated as they were drilled on its contents. Today, however, the book of Acts is somewhat neglected.

Acts is a narrative of early church history – but who really wants to read history, right? Yet, there's something mystical, sublime and enchanting about the contents of this New Testament book. The book of Acts is not simply a record of the activities of the early church; it is the record of God's activities through the Christians of the early church. If we read Acts simply to learn some historical facts (like charting the missionary tours of Paul), we miss the real power of its message.

Every generation has the responsibility before God to reproduce biblical Christianity. Every practice, doctrine and belief must pass the scrutiny of the New Testament so that such things may not "exceed what is written, in order that no one of you might become arrogant in behalf of one against the other" (1 Corinthians 4:6).

One challenge the modern church faces is the recovery of her ancient courage. The early Christians were courageous. This courage was a natural outgrowth of their Christianity. They weren't intimidated by the powerful; the rich could not seduce them. They refused to compromise when threatened. These early Christians had the courage to jettison prejudicial attitudes and religious customs when such things were inconsistent with the spirit and teachings of Jesus Christ. This is not to say that they didn't make mistakes. They had their problems, but they sought ways to eliminate them. They were truly a courageous generation.

I have chosen the first 12 chapters of the book of Acts as my focus of study because the first decade of the church's existence was a critical period. By Acts chapter 13, the early church had reached maturity, although a conference was called (Acts 15) to rehash and settle once and for all an earlier dispute. Acts 1-12 contains important principles necessary to the revitalization of courage in the modern church. It is the aim of this book to rekindle the fire of courageous Christianity to meet the challenges we face in the 21st century.

Dr. G. Scott Gleaves
Tallahassee, Fla.
2004

Chapter 1

The Courage to Believe

Acts 1:1-11

"Now, God be prais'd, that to believing souls
Gives light in darkness, comfort in despair!"
Shakespeare *(King Henry, the Sixth, II, i, 66)*

Kamikaze in Japanese means "divine wind." During World War II, Japan sent an elite special air force against her enemies. This special force had only one mission. It was a mission of no return. It was a mission with one chance for success. It was a suicide mission. When the kamikaze pilots spotted the enemy, they crashed their planes into the Allied warships on the water below. In defense against our invasion of Okinawa the Japanese used more than 6,000 suicide planes.

What motivated such sacrifice and determination? The answer is found in the word "kamikaze." Each pilot, convinced of the divine purpose of the goal, carried out his mission to completion. The kamikaze pilots believed eternal rewards awaited them.

The Power of Belief

There is power in believing. Arnold Toynbee once stated, "Apathy can be overcome by enthusiasm," and one way enthusiasm can be aroused is by "an idea, which takes the imagination by storm." A captivating idea will compel us to achieve beyond our expectations.

The story about the tower of Babel when God confounded the languages of the people illustrates the power of belief (Genesis 11:1-9). After God destroyed the ancient world with a flood, He commanded Noah and his family to repopulate the earth. The succeeding generations, however, decided to commune together and build a great city with a tower reaching high into the sky. They wanted to make a name for themselves, and they would have succeeded if God had not intervened and hindered their rebellious project. One thing is clear, when people really believe in something, they will work feverishly to achieve their goals.

What if the motivation fueled by the power of belief could somehow be channeled toward a worthy goal? What if we could capture that force and direct it in the ways of God? What would happen if we were to discover a cure for all humanity's problems? How would we behave if we knew for a fact that our discovery would impact the lives of every human being for good? If we were convinced and knew it would make a profound difference, nothing would stop us from sharing our discovery with every person we meet.

Does such a profound discovery really exist? You bet it does! The discovery making such an impact upon both the modern and the ancient world is the truth that the Lord Jesus, crucified more than 2,000 years ago, still lives.

God Raised Him Up

Acts 1:1-11 charts the course for what follows throughout the book of Acts. Luke, the inspired writer, wrote about the mighty acts of God and their effects on first-century Christians with a special emphasis upon the trustworthiness of the resurrection of Jesus Christ.

The book of Acts shows how God's people carried out the Great Commission as they went into the world and preached the good news (Matthew 28:18-20). The early Christians preached the gospel first in Jerusalem and then branched out to other regions until the news of the resurrection had infiltrated every part of the known world. They were able to turn the world upside down because they believed Jesus was alive. Although Jesus was crucified, the early disciples knew He was raised from the dead by the power of God and by that same power was declared to be the Son of God (Romans 1:4).

The resurrection is the foundation of the Christian faith. Certainly, if the resurrection were a hoax, it would be absurd to discuss the actions of such a pitiful band of people. Consider the consequences if Jesus had not been raised from the dead:

> But if there is no resurrection of the dead, not even Christ has been raised; and if Christ has not been raised, then our preaching is vain, your faith also is vain. Moreover we are even found to be false witnesses of God, because we witnessed against God that He raised Christ, whom He did not raise, if in fact the dead are not raised. For if the dead are not raised, not even Christ has been raised; and if Christ has not been raised, your faith is worthless; you are still in your sins. Then those also who have fallen asleep in Christ have perished. If we have hoped in Christ in this life only, we are of all men most to be pitied (1 Corinthians 15:13-19).

The resurrection is not false – it's truth. Have we really internalized its significance? Do we begin each new day impressed with the fact that Jesus is alive? Does it make any difference in our lives? The degree of our motivation in service to God may be related to the degree of our belief in the resurrection.

People who believe in the risen Lord truly possess a fire that burns within them. Peter and John had the fire within them. After being threatened by the religious leaders not to speak any more in the name of Jesus Christ, Peter and John said they could not stop proclaiming what they had seen and heard. Christians can recapture such motivation and courage today.

Jesus Really Died

A lack of motivation in Christian service may be an indication of skepticism concerning Christ's resurrection. Truly the Christian walks by faith and not by sight (2 Corinthians 5:7), but there is an abundance of evidence substantiating the claim that Jesus lives.

The holy book of the Islamic faith, the Koran, teaches that Jesus feigned death – only appearing to be dead (Surah IV:157). Some people have picked up on this idea and have developed what is known as the "swoon theory." This theory suggests Jesus merely passed out while hanging on the cross and later revived in the cool tomb of Joseph. Because certain people attempt to dismiss the resurrection in such a fashion, let's begin with the evidence demonstrating Jesus to have actually died on the cross.

Before Jesus was crucified, His body suffered severely. It was customary for criminals condemned under Roman law to be scourged. The back of Jesus was stretched, and a Roman soldier whipped it until there was nothing left but frayed bloody tissue. Jesus also received blows of mockery to the head by a reed and blows to the face by open hands. A thorny crown was thrust upon His head. No wonder Jesus, when forced to carry His cross to Golgotha, collapsed beneath it (Matthew 27:27-31; Mark 15:15-19; John 19:1-3).

While on the cross, the agony didn't become less painful; it intensified. After driving the nails into His hands and feet, the executioners offered Jesus wine mixed with myrrh, a mixture that served as a type of painkiller, but Jesus refused it. Later, however, Jesus took some "sour wine" to quench His thirst. Finally, after hanging on the cross for about six hours, Jesus uttered a loud cry and died. To make sure those crucified were dead by sunset on Friday, the beginning of the Jewish Sabbath, Roman soldiers would break the legs of those still alive to hasten their deaths. When they came to Jesus, He was already dead, so His bones were not broken. A soldier pierced His side with a spear and blood and water came forth (Mark 15:23-37; John 19:30-34).

The events after Jesus' death on the cross are significant as well. Joseph of Arimathea asked Pilate for the body of Jesus to be given to him. Before Pilate released the body, he made sure Jesus was really dead. Receiving the news that He was, Pilate gave the body to Joseph. Immediately, the body of Jesus was wrapped in a linen cloth with about 100 pounds of spices and placed in a tomb. Joseph rolled a large stone in front of the opening to seal it (Mark 15:43-46; John 19:39-42).

When the events that happened before, during and after the crucifixion are combined, the evidence overwhelmingly confirms Jesus' death.

Some Who Saw Him

Now we are ready to consider the evidence for the resurrection of Jesus from the dead. Luke informs his readers how Jesus presented

Himself alive to many. Granted, if only a few people had claimed to see the resurrected Christ, there might be cause for skepticism. But Jesus appeared to multitudes of people. Among the people who saw Him were Mary Magdalene, James and the apostles. On one occasion, Jesus appeared to more than 500 people at once (Matthew 28:1-9; Mark 16:9; John 20:16-18; 1 Corinthians 15:5-7). These witnesses were not hallucinating or seeing some kind of phantom; there were too many of them. The evidence is clear – Jesus lives again!

The resurrection appearances occurred during a 40-day period giving skeptics ample time to investigate its truthfulness. The number "40" seems to be a significant number in the Bible. During the days of Noah, God caused rain to fall upon the earth for 40 days and 40 nights. Israel's punishment for failing to take the Promised Land was to wander in the wilderness for 40 years. In the New Testament, Jesus fasted for 40 days before Satan came to tempt Him, and He showed Himself alive for 40 days (Genesis 7:12; Numbers 14:33-34; Matthew 4:2).

Why the number 40 in all four cases? Because in each case, 40 represented a sufficient period of time. Forty days and nights of constant rainfall produced a sufficient amount of water to bring an end to all flesh. Forty years served as sufficient punishment for Israel's sin of unbelief, and 40 days represented a sufficient period of fasting. The number of days Jesus presented Himself alive was sufficient to cast out all doubt. Even doubting Thomas, after his investigation, exclaimed, "My Lord and my God" (John 20:26-29).

Jesus Is Lord

The power of the resurrection is illustrated in three ways. First, the position Jesus now holds is a display of the power of His resurrection. Three times Luke tells us Jesus was taken up or lifted up. Jesus was taken up into heaven, where He now reigns at the right hand of God (Hebrews 1:3). Because of His elevated position, Jesus claims to have all authority. As heaven encompasses the earth, the rule of Christ Jesus encompasses all lands and peoples. This being true, the gospel was to spread to the "remotest part of the earth."

Second, the nature of the kingdom is another display of the power of the resurrection. Forty references to God's kingdom (Greek, *basileia*) are in the Gospel of Luke and eight in the book of Acts. Clearly, the kingdom is a central theme in Luke's inspired writings. The resurrection gives new meaning to the concept of the kingdom. Much of what Jesus taught His disciples during the 40 days after His resurrection related to the kingdom. It was natural, therefore, for them to question Jesus about the arrival of the kingdom before He ascended into heaven.

The disciples thought the kingdom was literal. Their Jewish heritage caused them to long for an age when God's people would one day repossess the Promised Land and restore its glory to Israel. To their surprise, Jesus quickly dismissed their question and talked about the mission that He had for them – to be witnesses to the world. The disciples would soon realize the kingdom was a spiritual kingdom (John 18:36).

A third display of the power of the resurrection would be seen in the coming of the Holy Spirit. Jesus promised His disciples He was going to send them the Holy Spirit in a few days. The Holy Spirit's arrival would mark the fulfillment of God's promise and would begin a new era in God's dealings with humankind.

The purpose behind the coming of the Holy Spirit, Jesus stated, was to empower the apostles. You might ask, "The power to do what?" Jesus had previously told His disciples "repentance for the forgiveness of sins" was to be proclaimed in His name beginning in Jerusalem (Luke 24:46-47). To be specially prepared to do this, they were to wait until they received power to make them complete. The Holy Spirit would come to lead them into all truth, whereby they would be empowered to be true and faithful witnesses (John 14:23-24; 16:12-13).

Promises Kept

Two promises are connected to the resurrection of Jesus. The first promise is the return of Jesus. If we believe Jesus was raised from the dead, we also know He is one day coming to receive His own:

> Let not your heart be troubled; believe in God, believe also in Me. In My Father's house are many dwelling places; if it were not so, I would have told you; for I go to prepare a place for you. And if I go and prepare a place for you, I will come again, and receive you to Myself; that where I am, there you may be also (John 14:1-3).

As the disciples stood gazing into the sky, two angels appeared and reassured them, "This Jesus, who has been taken up ... into heaven, will come in just the same way as you have watched Him go into heaven" (Acts 1:11; 1 Thessalonians 4:13-18; 2 Thessalonians 1:7-9). The resurrection fortifies us with perseverance to live faithfully for Jesus knowing we shall see Him one sweet day.

The second promise is the assurance of victory. Because Jesus overcame the greatest power of Satan – death – we can now have confidence in our own personal victory over sin, suffering and death. Whatever evils may come our way, through faith in Christ Jesus we can be victorious. The words of the song, "Because He Lives," illustrate the assurance we derive from Christ's resurrection:

God sent His Son,
They called Him Jesus,
He came to love, heal, and forgive;
He lived and died to buy my pardon,
An empty grave is there to prove my Savior lives.

How sweet to hold a newborn baby,
And feel the pride, and joy He gives;
But greater still the calm assurance,
This child can face uncertain days because He lives.

And then one day I'll cross that river,
I'll fight life's final war with pain;
And then as death gives way to vict'ry,
I'll see the lights of glory and I'll know He lives.

Because He lives I can face tomorrow,
Because He lives all fear is gone;
Because I know He holds the future,
And life is worth the living just because He lives.

Now, what have you decided? Do you have the courage to believe Jesus lives?

Power Thoughts for Group Discussion

1. What other biblical and secular examples illustrate the power of belief?

2. What impact has the truth of Jesus' resurrection had upon the ancient and modern world? What impact has the resurrection had upon you personally?

3. Discuss other evidences that confirm the truthfulness of the resurrection.

4. Thomas doubted the testimony of the other apostles concerning the resurrection. Was his doubting good or bad? Explain.

5. "The degree of our motivation in service to God may be related to the degree of our belief in the resurrection." Do you agree or disagree with this statement? Why or why not?

Chapter 2

The Courage to Grow

Acts 1:12-26

*"Man matures through work
which inspires him to difficult good."*
John Paul II

Skip, my stepfather, was just 43 years old. He was in the best of shape. He and I loved doing outdoor activities together – fishing, working in the yard, and playing with our dog, Coco. I've never met another person who was more endearing. Skip had defeated cancer 10 years earlier but thought it might be back. His thoughts jumped around as he paced back and forth in the doctor's examining room. His suspicions were correct. "Skip, I'm sorry," said the doctor matter-of-factly, "but you have pancreatic cancer." Then came the dreaded prognosis: "You only have about six months to live." It now looked as if the disease would ultimately be victorious. Skip lived for 18 months, but his suffering and treatments made his life miserable.

"You have six months to live." It sounds so horrible and threatening, doesn't it? These words have a ring of finality. Maybe that's the reason we fear them. How can we avoid the inevitable? We can't. About all that can be done is to make sure everything is in order before the end comes. Skip did exactly that. He left nothing undone.

Loose Ends

In the Old Testament, God told King Hezekiah to get his house in order. Hezekiah had been suffering from an illness and inquired of God what he should expect the outcome to be. "You're going to die," God said (2 Kings 20:1). In effect, God was telling Hezekiah he needed to tie up any loose ends beforehand.

Haven't we had to make sure things were in order before we embarked on a vacation or some other trip? Arrangements must be made for someone to feed the dog, look after the house, and pick up the newspaper from the front yard. We like knowing everything is in order before we leave.

Acts 1:12-26 is insightful. From all appearances, the disciples seem to be conducting a simple business meeting. However, this was no ordinary business meeting. The disciples were making special preparations and tying up loose ends to be ready when the Holy Spirit would descend upon them, as Jesus had promised. In this meeting, the disciples were facing and striving to overcome their weaknesses. If we are going to meet the challenges awaiting us, we must overcome and rise above our own weaknesses. The disciples turned six weaknesses into strengths that day.

Strong in Faith

The first weakness the disciples addressed was their faith. Many had assembled together during the 10-day period between the ascension of Jesus and the Day of Pentecost. Among those who had assembled were the apostles (less Judas Iscariot) and the biological half-brothers of Jesus, all of whom at one time or another were extremely weak in faith.

After Jesus had calmed a storm on the Sea of Galilee, He rebuked His disciples saying, "Where is your faith?" (Luke 8:25). Later, the disciples asked Jesus to help them increase their faith. The Gospel of Mark is filled with comments about how faithless the apostles were (Mark 4:40; 6:6, 52; 8:21). All the apostles, you remember, scattered when the Jewish leaders arrested Jesus in the Garden of Gethsemane. Who could forget the denials of Peter, the rugged fisherman? But where are the apostles now? They are together and aware of their weaknesses. They were now determined more than ever to grow in their faith.

The faith of Jesus' brothers was also weak. In the beginning they were skeptical about the divinity of Jesus. When Jesus went to Nazareth, His hometown, they rejected His claims of being the Messiah (Mark 6:1-6). On one occasion, His brothers ridiculed Him. They jeered and said if He was indeed who He claimed to be, He should go to Jerusalem and show Himself to the people. In essence, they were saying to Jesus, "Stop being so secretive about the whole thing" (John 7:1-5); now His brothers were also at this special business meeting. They were no longer skeptics, but believers. Later, James would become one of the undisputed pillars of the church. God would also use James to write an epistle bearing his name. The opening verse of James' book leaves no doubt as to the status of his faith: "James, a bond-servant of ... Jesus Christ" (James 1:1). He could have written, "James, the brother of Jesus," but he didn't. Why? Because he knew his primary relationship to Jesus was not physical but spiritual. He believed Jesus was his Lord and Savior.

The apostles and the brothers of Jesus were together. In the past they had been very weak, but now their faith was strong.

An Untapped Resource

The second weakness addressed by the disciples concerned the ministry of women. Not only were Jesus' apostles and brothers present in the gathering, but we also read about some women who were there. Their presence is significant. Under the strict legal system of Judaism, women were suppressed. Because their burden was so severe, women felt a great sense of liberation in the teachings of Jesus.

In his writings, Luke places special emphasis upon the ministry of women in the life of Jesus. They were not just bystanders; they were actively involved in the plans of God. God sent the angel Gabriel to Mary and Zecharias, the husband of Elizabeth, with spectacular news (Luke 1:11-20, 26-27). While Jesus was dining in a Pharisee's house, a woman rushed in holding an alabaster vial of expensive perfume to use in anointing Jesus' feet. Simon sneered at her actions, but Jesus used the incident to teach him a lesson about gratitude (7:36-47). During the ministry of Jesus, some prominent women supported Him and His disciples financially (8:1-3).

The church needs the involvement of women. A certain flavor is added to the work of the church when women are appreciated for the works they do. Women possess special qualities, adding a unique yet essential dimension to the church's ministry. Paul wrote how a woman should not "exercise authority over a man." However, he continued to say how a woman would be preserved through the bearing of children, only if she lived a life of faith, love, purity and devotion. The phrase, "bearing of children," describes a distinctive role or part women play that men cannot. In fulfilling their role, women bring honor and glory to God (1 Timothy 2:12-15).

When we consider the distinctive part women play in the church, at least two qualities surface. Women usually possess these qualities in a greater degree than do men. God has endowed the spirit of womanhood with a tremendous capacity for patience. Even Paul, when writing to the young church in Thessalonica, described his actions among them as a "nursing mother who tenderly cares for her children" (1 Thessalonians 2:7). Have you noticed the Bible always exhorts fathers not to discourage or provoke their children (Ephesians 6:4; Colossians 3:21)? Could it be fathers generally are not as patient with their children as are mothers? Much could be learned from the patience of women. God desires His people to be patient with one another. When there is trouble in the church, we need to be patient. The same holds true in whatever circumstance we find ourselves.

Another quality women possess in a greater degree than men is compassion. We become more like Jesus when we exemplify a compassionate attitude. Jesus was concerned about the welfare of others. When Peter was on his way to Cornelius' house, he stopped at Lydda when he heard about a woman who had died. It was brought to Peter's attention all Dorcas had made with her hands. It was evident Dorcas lived a very compassionate life – look at all she had done for others. Her attitude is commendable. The garments were the fruits of her compassion (Acts 9:39).

Patience and compassion are desperately needed in the lives of Christians. Women exhibit these special qualities. Therefore, we should support and encourage godly women. Preparing ourselves for the challenges awaiting us will require a greater appreciation for the ministry of women.

The Power of Prayer

The third weakness was the manner in which the disciples had been praying. When the disciples of Jesus were meeting together, Luke wrote about their devoting themselves to prayer. We recall Jesus had appeared to many people during a period of 40 days. They witnessed the resurrected Lord and even saw His ascension. Prayer had now taken on a whole new meaning. The disciples had a deeper appreciation for the power of prayer and the comfort it provided. How could they keep from praying? Too many wonderful things had happened. Jesus was now in heaven with the Father, and the uniform consensus of the group was, "Let's pray."

The church throughout the book of Acts is pictured as a praying church (Acts 2:42; 4:31; 12:5, 12). Prayer solidifies the church. The communication lines between heaven and earth are open. We cannot afford to neglect prayer; we must pray without ceasing (1 Thessalonians 5:17).

God's Word Is True

The fourth weakness was the disciples' attitude toward holy Scripture. Peter stood up and explained that Scripture had to be fulfilled. In the Psalms, God foretold about the apostasy of Judas. The disciples were overwhelmed by the trustworthiness of God's will as revealed in Scripture. Peter alluded to two Old Testament passages to show it was necessary to select another man to replace Judas as an apostle (Psalms 69:25; 109:8). The disciples had read these passages many times but now finally understood their profound meaning – like a light bulb clicking on in their minds. The whole redemptive plan of God came together so easily now. "It's all right here in the Scripture!" they may have said to one another.

When David composed these psalms, he didn't realize God was revealing events to occur years later. On the surface, David wrote about his enemies and God's judgment against them. These psalms, however, contained an inner meaning, and now the disciples understood it. Concerning the Word of God, Peter wrote, "'All flesh is like grass; And all its glory like the flower of grass. The grass withers, And the flower falls off, But the word of the Lord abides forever' " (1 Peter 1:24-25). A profound respect for the Word of God is essential to the ministry of the church.

God Is in Control

The fifth weakness the disciples faced dealt with the matter of God's sovereignty. After Peter described the qualifications of an apostle, the group set forward two men as possible candidates, Barsabbas (Justus) and Matthias. Recognizing that only God knew the hearts of people, the disciples consulted Him through an offering of prayer. From all appearances, these two men were equally qualified to replace Judas. The selection between the two was God's decision to make. He alone knew who would be the better choice (1 Chronicles 28:9; Jeremiah 17:10).

The disciples cast lots, and the lot fell on Matthias. The casting of lots was a Jewish practice of determining the will of God; it was not an action of chance or a gamble. This practice cannot be compared to flipping coins or drawing straws. God directly influenced the outcome of the lot. This is the last reference to casting lots in the Bible. The Holy Spirit would soon descend upon the apostles and guide them into all truth (John 14:24-25; 16:12-13). The Holy Spirit would also guide the writers of the New Testament so men and women everywhere in every century would be able to discover God's will for their lives (2 Timothy 3:15-17; 2 Peter 1:3).

On occasion we may assume we already know God's will. Several people in the Bible once thought they knew, too, and later lived to regret it. Peter is a perfect example. He often assumed he knew the right thing to do. Such presumption received a scathing rebuke from Jesus (Mark 8:33). The disciples had now come to respect God's sovereignty. Through prayer and the casting of lots, they yielded to God's sovereignty over the lives of His people. Where God was to lead, they were to follow. Today, through prayer and the study of Scripture, we also can determine the course we must take for our lives.

A Warning to All

The sixth weakness the disciples addressed was the danger of falling away from God. Judas had all the advantages. He was selected to be an apostle; he experienced first hand the many truths Jesus taught and the profound things He did. Judas was personally familiar with the power of God because he, along with the other apostles, could perform miracles. He had it made except for one major problem – Judas was vulnerable to the enticements of Satan. Judas' weakness was money. He often pilfered the money box supporting Jesus and the other apostles (John 12:6). He even sold himself to betray the Lord for 30 pieces of silver (Matthew 26:15; 27:3, 9). Instead of asking for help and fighting to overcome the temptations of Satan, Judas quietly lusted for more and more until he finally lost control. He later realized what he had done, but instead of seeking forgiveness, he took his own life (v. 5).

Judas stands as a powerful reminder of the possibility of falling away from God. It's not a probability; it's just a possibility. There will be those who, like Judas, will betray the Lord Jesus. Knowing this possibility exists should cause us to be alert and watchful lest we be overcome by the deceitfulness of sin. Paul warned the elders of the church in Ephesus about a time when men would arise among them and begin to lead many astray (Acts 20:30).

Paul encourages restoration to those who are overtaken in a transgression (Galatians 6:1). If the possibility did not exist, it would be senseless for Paul to give such an exhortation. Restoration implies an apostasy. James, likewise, says there are those among us who will fall away. A large part of a Christian's job is the reclamation of those who have gone astray (James 5:19-20; 2 Peter 3:17).

Minutes of the Meeting

As we have already observed, the meeting in Acts 1 was not ordinary. Jesus' disciples were facing their weaknesses head on and doing something about them. Their efforts were preparing them for the awesome challenges soon to await them. If they were going to meet those challenges and march forward in the cause of Christ, they had to tie up loose ends. Are we ready to face the challenges and the opportunities awaiting us? We will only be ready if we take the time to strengthen our weaknesses. We may have to work harder at strengthening the following areas: our faith, the ministry of women, the priority of prayer, our respect for God's inspired Word, our submission to the sovereignty of God, and our awareness of apostasy.

Power Thoughts for Group Discussion

1. Jesus often rebuked His disciples for having little faith. What did Jesus mean by this? What are the characteristics of little faith?

2. Discuss the special contributions women make to the work of the church. How can the ministry of women be strengthened in your congregation?

3. How is the sovereignty of God played out in the lives of Christians? Does the sovereignty of God rule out freedom of will?

4. Read James 1:13-15. Describe how and why a Christian might stray from God.

5. Make a list of your congregation's strengths and weaknesses. What specific actions could be taken to strengthen the weaknesses?

Chapter 3

The Courage to Follow

Acts 2:1-12

*"To change your mind and to follow him who sets
you right is to be nonetheless the free agent
that you were before."*
Marcus Aurelius

My wife and I just purchased a sofa and love seat. They are beautiful. Their rich and bright colors will provide the perfect accent to an otherwise bland living room. However, it's going to take at least two weeks before our new furniture is delivered. That's a problem because we want our furniture now. We don't want to wait for it. We're tired of looking at our old furniture, and we're excited about the arrival of the new.

It is difficult to wait when we are anticipating the arrival of something special. Time moves slowly for a student anticipating his graduation. When a child's birthday draws near, it's all he can do to contain himself. I can remember counting those unusually long days until Christmas. My excitement grew just thinking about Santa Claus, candy and lots of toys.

Anticipation!

Think for a moment about the excitement building within the disciples as they anticipated the coming of the Holy Spirit. Jesus told them the Holy Spirit would come "not many days from now." Since the ascension of Jesus into heaven, the disciples had been praying together, eagerly awaiting the arrival of the Holy Spirit. The disciples surely had many questions about the Holy Spirit. Some of their questions might have been something like: "What will the coming of the Holy Spirit mean?" "What will He do when He arrives?" "What role will He have in the age of the Messiah?"

According to Acts 2, the Holy Spirit played an important role in the formation of a redeemed community of people – the church. The Holy Spirit achieved four goals when He came on that first Pentecost after the resurrection of Jesus. These same four goals continue to express our fundamental purpose today.

Why the Holy Spirit Came

The Holy Spirit's descent came on a special Jewish feast day called Pentecost. When the Holy Spirit arrived, He achieved His first goal – getting people's attention. Pentecost means "50." This celebration occurred 50 days after the Sabbath of the Passover. Consequently, Pentecost always fell on the "first day of the week." This great feast commemorated the first fruits of harvest. Multitudes of Jews and proselytes made the journey to Jerusalem to participate in the festivities.

The coming of the Holy Spirit served a threefold purpose. First, His coming marked the beginning of a new era in God's dealings with humanity. After God delivered the Israelites from the bondage of Egypt, He guided them to Mount Sinai. The Israelites marveled at the spectacular sight of God's descent upon the mountain. From the midst of the flashing of lightning and clapping of thunder, God first spoke to the people directly, but because His voice generated fear in them, Moses ascended the mountain to intercede. Acts 2, like Exodus, began a new era in God's redemptive plan.

Second, the Holy Spirit's arrival revealed God's presence in Jerusalem. Luke wrote that the Holy Spirit's entry into the world was like a violent wind. As a result of being filled with the Holy Spirit, there appeared something like tongues of fire resting upon the heads of the apostles. It was obvious these phenomena were of divine origin because these uneducated, Galilean fishermen were able to speak in other languages "as the Spirit [gave] them utterance."

Galileans had a unique dialect, and everyone recognized their speech. A woman recognized Peter's Galilean characteristics while he warmed himself by a fire during the trial of Jesus (Matthew 26:73). The miraculous ability the apostles had to speak in other languages reversed the curse given at the tower of Babel (Genesis 11:1-9). There, God halted the purpose of the people by confusing their language. At Pentecost, God united people by communicating the gospel in the languages of those present.

The third reason the Holy Spirit came, and most likely the main reason on this occasion, was to spark curiosity. Notice how the people responded to what they saw and heard; they were "bewildered" (Acts 2:6) and "amazed" (v. 7). Luke continues, "And they continued in amazement and great perplexity, saying to one another, 'What does this mean?' " (v. 12). Such perplexity was exactly what God wanted everyone's response to be. Because the people were now filled with curiosity, it was time to tell those gathered what all of these things meant.

Good News for the Lost

After successfully accomplishing the first goal of getting everyone's attention, the Holy Spirit, through the agency of the apostles, achieved His second goal – delivering God's message of salvation. This message contained a number of gripping truths. When Peter stood up with the 11, he laid to rest the accusation he and the other apostles were inebriated. To the contrary, the events unfolding fulfilled the words of Joel's prophecy spoken almost 800 years before this event (Joel 2:28-32).

Acts 2:21 is the heart and soul of God's news to humankind: "And it shall be, that everyone who calls on the name of the Lord shall be saved." The Bible is the book on salvation. In Genesis 3:15, God told Satan the seed of woman would crush his head. Paul identified the seed of woman as Jesus (Galatians 4:4). When Jesus was raised from the dead, Satan, metaphorically, received an incurable blow to the head (Hebrews 2:14-15). Therefore, deliverance (salvation) from sin is found in Jesus Christ (John 3:16).

Peter's sermon on salvation assumes those who heard it were lost (Romans 3:23; 6:23). Therefore, each person was accountable, as the word "everyone" in Joel's prophecy implied. We stand or fall as individuals before God. The salvation of our souls is dependent upon our personal response to the gospel. This message of hope proves the accessibility of salvation for every person. Anyone can choose to call upon the name of the Lord. There is for us a way to have our sin-stained souls cleansed. Calling upon the name of the Lord provides the way. The name "Jesus" means "salvation," and to call on His name is to appeal to Him as the source and the provider of salvation. Calling leads inevitably to obedience (Hebrews 5:8-9).

Jesus Is Like No Other

Because Jesus was raised from the dead, His resurrection becomes the guarantee of salvation. Peter follows four lines of evidence proving Jesus was not a mere man.

Consider first the person of Jesus. Peter said, "Men of Israel, listen to these words: Jesus the Nazarene, a man attested to you by God with miracles and wonders and signs which God performed through Him in your midst, just as you yourselves know" (Acts 2:22). Jesus performed many extraordinary acts attesting to the truth that He was different. He was Immanuel, which means, "God with us." The miracles He performed were in plain view for all to see. As Paul once told most excellent Festus, these things were not done "in a corner" (26:26).

Second, the fulfillment of Old Testament prophecy was another reason substantiating the divinity of Jesus. Peter alluded to three of David's psalms. Psalm 16:8-11 focused upon David's feelings of anguish and the reassurance of knowing God would help him in the fight against his enemies. This psalm, however, is used by Peter to show how its deeper meaning foreshadowed the resurrection of Jesus. Jesus' body did not undergo decay, but arose from the tomb on the third day. This passage was not a reference to David; because he died and his bones were still in the grave.

In Psalm 132:11, God promised to set one of David's descendants upon his throne. Jesus Christ fulfilled this promise because Jesus was a descendant of King David. Psalm 110:1 verifies David as a prophet. He prophesied how the Lord (God the Father) said unto David's Lord (the Son of God – Jesus) that He (the Son) would sit at His (the Father's) right hand (Hebrews 1:3). This psalm had nothing to do with the exaltation of

David. Peter, therefore, demonstrates with great clarity how one of the esteemed heroes of Israel, David, pointed to Christ's exaltation.

The third line of evidence Peter followed was based upon the testimony of eyewitnesses. As noted in Chapter 1, multitudes had not only seen the miracles performed by Jesus, but also had seen His post-resurrection appearances.

Finally, Peter mentioned the presence of the Holy Spirit was yet another proof of Jesus' divinity. The audience couldn't deny the things they had seen and heard. There was only one conclusion: "Therefore let all the house of Israel know for certain that God has made Him both Lord and Christ – this Jesus whom you crucified" (Acts 2:36). What a climax to the Holy Spirit's message of salvation.

What Must We Do, Lord?

The Holy Spirit's third goal after delivering God's message to the people was to convict them of sin. Acts 2:37 records how the message affected those who heard it. Luke wrote they were "pierced" through the heart. They were convicted of their sins. Jesus told His disciples earlier one of the main purposes of the Holy Spirit's work was to convict the world of sin (John 16:8). Their question reveals that Peter's message accomplished God's intended purpose. All who have become disciples of Jesus have first had their hearts pierced by the message of the cross, leading them to ask, "What shall we do?"

The question implies the inquirer understood there would be conditions of pardon. Peter commanded them to repent and be baptized to obtain ("for") the remission of sins. To repent is to "make a change," to "turn." One who repents is essentially saying, "From this point forward, I'm turning from sin and will do what pleases the Lord" (cf. Romans 6:12-13; 1 Thessalonians 1:9). The importance of repentance cannot be over emphasized because no unrepentant soul shall have a place in the kingdom of heaven (Luke 24:45-47; 2 Peter 3:9).

Baptism is likewise essential to the salvation of our souls. Baptism is an outward demonstration of an inward crucifixion of self (Romans 6:1-6). After baptism, we are raised to walk in newness of life. Many people disregard baptism as a condition of salvation, but that is the very thing Peter told them to do. Paul still retained his sins until he was told by Ananias, "Arise, and be baptized, and wash away your sins" (Acts 22:16). Those people touched by the gospel should be required to do no less and no more than what the Holy Spirit ordered as the conditions of pardon. God by His grace offers us the opportunity to be saved, but we must obey His conditions of pardon.

Notice the connection between Peter's answer in Acts 2:38 and the theme of salvation contained in his sermon in Acts 2:21. As stated earlier, those who repented and were baptized received the remission of sins as promised. Sin separates people from God (Isaiah 59:1-2), and to obtain the remission of sins is to have fellowship with God restored. Isaiah described a soul cleansed from sin when he wrote: "Though your sins are as scarlet, They will be as white as snow; Though they are red like crimson, they will be like wool" (1:18).

Peter continued to show if the opportunity was seized upon, not only would there be forgiveness of sins, but we would also receive the indwelling of the Holy Spirit in our lives. Later, Peter affirmed that God gives the Holy Spirit to all who obey Him. This indwelling serves as a pledge of our inheritance (Ephesians 1:13-14). Because our bodies house the Spirit, we are to live holy and godly lives consistent with the Holy Spirit's message. The indwelling of the Holy Spirit, then, verifies our salvation (Acts 5:32; 1 Corinthians 6:19-20).

Another connecting link to salvation is seen in Acts 2:41. About 3,000 souls were added to the body of believers on the Day of Pentecost. This group represented God's kingdom, the church (Colossians 1:13-14). God Himself added them to the church. How appropriate it was for the Holy Spirit to descend on this glorious day. While the Jews celebrated the first fruits of their physical harvest, God celebrated the first fruits of His spiritual harvest (compare John 14:24-25; 16:12-13).

Guided by the Spirit

The fourth goal of the Holy Spirit's arrival was to lead believers in God's way. Much confusion exists in the religious world as to how the Spirit leads people. Jesus succinctly declared the method or means used – the Word or Scripture. The Holy Spirit would guide the apostles into all truth by bringing to their remembrance all Jesus taught and showing them further revelations from Christ. The teachings of the apostles, therefore, were the teachings of the Holy Spirit (God). Peter's words are illustrative: "But know this first of all, that no prophecy of Scripture is a matter of one's own interpretation, for no prophecy was ever made by an act of human will, but men moved by the Holy Spirit spoke from God" (2 Peter 1:20-21). The apostles were special ambassadors of Jesus Christ.

How do we really know if the Holy Spirit is leading us? There are three indicators of the Holy Spirit's leading.

• *Behavior.* The first indicator of whether a person is being led by the Holy Spirit is to look at the fruit (or behavior) of the individual who claims to be a Christian. Those who became Christians, Luke writes, were devoted to the apostles' teachings. They understood that the Spirit was leading them through the apostles' word, and subsequently, through their divinely inspired written word (1 Corinthians 4:6; Ephesians 3:3-4). The Holy Spirit, therefore, guides not by subjective phenomena, but by objective truth preserved in the Bible. What is the fruit of your behavior?

• *Unity.* Second, unity among the disciples is another fruit revealing the Holy Spirit's guidance. The disciples enjoyed fellowship; they were constantly together; they had all things in common; they shared what they had with others; and they possessed a singleness of mind. This unity was consistent with the prayer of Jesus recorded in John 17:15-23:

> I do not ask Thee to take them out of the world, but to keep them from the evil one. They are not of the world, even as I am not of the world. Sanctify them in the truth; Thy word is truth. As Thou didst send Me into the world, I also have sent them into the world. And for their sakes I sanctify Myself, that they themselves also may be sanctified in truth. I do not ask in behalf of these alone, but for those also who believe in Me through their word; that they may all be one; even as Thou, Father, art in Me, and I in Thee, that they also may be in Us; that the world may believe that Thou didst send Me. And the glory which Thou hast given Me I have given to them; that they may be one, just as We are one; I in them, and Thou in Me, that they may be perfected in uni-

ty, that the world may know that Thou didst send Me, and didst love them, even as Thou didst love Me.

Later, however, the church lost much of its unity (1 Corinthians 1:10) because of its failure to follow the Holy Spirit's teachings. How is your relationship with other Christians?

• *Determination.* A third fruit revealing how the Holy Spirit was leading these early Christians can be seen in their passionate determination to please and to praise God. These were not lukewarm Christians. Their ambition was to please God and to bring glory to Him (Matthew 6:33). Following the lead of the Holy Spirit today will produce the same results. Where is God on your list of priorities?

Following the Spirit

Conflict between the Spirit-led life and the Satan-led life permeates the book of Acts. A life guided by the Holy Spirit cannot be conquered. The church continued to expand and grow, even in the midst of extreme opposition, beyond any human comprehension (Acts 2:41; 4:4; 5:14). How do we follow the Holy Spirit's lead? Notice again the four goals the Holy Spirit achieved:

• The Spirit raised curiosity.
• The Spirit delivered God's message.
• The Spirit convicted people of sin.
• The Spirit led the believers who were saved.

A parallel does exist for us. When we rise from a restful night of sleep, what happens in our world as we begin a new day? Shouldn't our lives arrest curiosity in others? Is there really anything different about us in comparison to those who are of the world? Jesus often used metaphors such as "light" and "salt" to describe the distinctive lives His people are to live, lives causing others to take notice (Matthew 5:13-16; 1 Peter 3:15).

Just as the Holy Spirit delivered God's message, so our lives powerfully proclaim our love for Jesus to the people we meet. We are living letters to be read and known by all (2 Corinthians 3:3). Our lives should be a living message of hope as others see in us a spirit of joy even in the midst of adversity. As the people of the world observe our behavior, shouldn't they be convicted of sin and be motivated to pursue for themselves God's great opportunity of salvation (1 Peter 2:12; 3:1-2)?

In today's church, our devotion to the Word of God will manifest itself in unity – the kind where there exists a common and unbreakable bond between the members of God's family. Such unity and devotion would powerfully attest to the world that the story of the cross is true (John 17:21, 23).

The Holy Spirit of God made a powerful entry into the world. When we have the courage to follow His lead, our lives will have no less an impact upon the neighborhoods in which we live. "The best effort of a fine person," wrote Emerson, "is felt after we have left their presence." A valid question to ask then is: What effect has our presence had upon the lives of others?

Power Thoughts for Group Discussion

1. How does one call upon the name of the Lord? Read Acts 2:21 and Hebrews 5:8-9.

2. Is it possible to know whether or not a person has repented? What would be the criteria for making such a determination?

3. What can be learned from Paul's discussion of Christian baptism in Romans 6:1-6?

4. List the three ways found in this chapter illustrating the "leading of the Holy Spirit." Discuss how these relate to the "fruit of the Spirit" in Galatians 5:22-23.

5. Gary McIntosh and Glen Martin, in their book, *Finding Them, Keeping Them*, wrote: "Churches that are effectively reaching people for Christ see the needs of the unchurched, establish ministries that allow the church to be present in the community, and have a process by which they are able to draw these unchurched people into the safety of Christ and a local church" (22). What could your congregation do to make its presence better felt in the community?

Chapter 4

The Courage to Change

Acts 3:1-10

"God, give us grace to accept with serenity the things that cannot be changed, courage to change the things which should be changed, and the wisdom to distinguish the one from the other."
Reinhold Niebuhr, *The Serenity Prayer (1932)*

It was Friday night. I had prepared for this game all week. I had the jitters, but I was ready. I was the deep man on the kick-off return team. The whistle blew and the game started. The opening kick-off came right to me. I caught the football and started making my moves. Things were going my way that night because I charged forward for a touchdown. It was my moment of glory. "That was number 22," screamed the announcer, "Steve Gleaves."

My name isn't Steve Gleaves.

I have a brother by that name, but that's not my name. He is who he is, and I am who I am. And it wasn't Steve who made the touchdown; it was Scott!

Nothing in a Name?

That eventful night reminds me how dear my name is to me. It's normal for us to want people to pronounce and spell our names correctly. Names are more than tags that identify a person. A name encompasses the whole of an individual – it embodies his personality and character.

It is difficult for our culture to understand the significance of names as they were used during Bible times. Names were often given to children to symbolize some unusual event. For instance, Abraham and Sarah's son was named "Isaac," which means "to laugh." According to Genesis 18, God promised Abraham, despite the fact he and Sarah were very old, they would have a child. When Sarah overheard this statement from those men who visited Abraham, she laughed. The whole thing seemed too incredible; so later the child of promise received an appropriate name, Isaac. Earlier, God had changed Abram's name to Abraham (father of multitudes), and Sarai's name to Sarah (princess).

God believes His name is important, too. One of the Ten Commandments warns, "You shall not take the name of the Lord your God in vain" (Exodus 20:7). When the Israelites defiled the name of God by ungodly living, God defended His name by punishing them (Ezekiel 36:20-23).

The name given to the Son of God was not an accident either. The angel Gabriel told Joseph he was to call the son born to Mary, Jesus, "for it is He who will save His people from their sins." Jesus means "Savior" (Matthew 1:21). The name of Jesus possesses abundant honor and glory. Luke emphasizes the name of Jesus in Acts 3 and 4 (3:6, 16; 4:7-10, 12, 17-18, 30). Certainly the name of Jesus should be spoken with reverence and honor.

Perfect Health

Luke introduces Peter and John as they are going to the temple at about 3 o'clock in the afternoon. Sitting by the gate named Beautiful was a lame beggar. Crippled since birth, he was now 40 years old. At first glance, we're sympathetic toward his pitiful condition. The irony is that he portrays our pathetic spiritual condition. He couldn't walk, and neither can we. Like him, we are unable to help ourselves. Just as he was incapable of being healed by any human effort, our spiritual disease is likewise incurable. The only thing the beggar could do was rely upon the mercy of others for his survival (Isaiah 1:5; Jeremiah 10:23; Romans 7:24-25). Our spiritual dependence is no different.

Having fixed their gaze upon him, Peter and John said to the beggar, "Look at us!" Naturally the beggar thought he was about to receive something from them, but it was not going to be what he expected. Peter then said, "I do not possess silver and gold, but what I do have I give to you: In the name of Jesus Christ the Nazarene – walk!" (Acts 3:6). Immediately the beggar received what the name only could provide – a cure. "And with a leap," Luke wrote, "he stood upright." The lame beggar couldn't keep still, but kept leaping about, rejoicing and praising God. The prophet Isaiah told of a time when the lame would "leap like a deer" (Isaiah 35:6). Here Isaiah's words are fulfilled. The age of the Messiah had arrived. The lame were made whole.

"Made well" in Acts 4:9 is translated from the same word as "saved" in Acts 4:12. The first reference is to a physical state and the second to a spiritual one. The point is: the lame beggar was made whole by the power of the name, and by the same name we are made spiritually whole. Just think of the new life this beggar had received. He now could walk, jump and run – things once out of his reach he now possessed. Because of the power of Jesus' name, the lame beggar enjoyed perfect health for the first time.

Paul states, "Therefore if any man is in Christ, he is a new creature; the old things passed away; behold, new things have come" (2 Corinthians 5:17). A new life is available to all. We can be "born again" (John 3:3-5). We can "walk in newness of life" (Romans 6:4). Jesus makes our rebirth possible.

Strong in the Lord

Peter and John's preaching drew persecution from members of the Jewish Council. Because the Council was primarily composed of a class known as the Sadducees, the apostles' teaching about a resurrection from the dead struck a sour chord. The Sadducees believed such teaching was nonsense, so Peter and John were thrown in jail.

Jesus taught His disciples to anticipate opposition coming in the form of threats or even physical abuse. "Remember the word that I said to you. 'A slave is not greater than his master.' If they persecuted Me, they will also persecute you" (John 15:20). Preaching in the name of Jesus will at times make enemies. Truth exposes error. Light exposes the deeds of darkness (3:19-20). The righteous actions of Abel exposed Cain's evil heart. Consequently, Cain slew his brother. When we attempt to live godly lives, it should not come as a surprise if we face hostility without provocation from others (Genesis 4; Hebrews 11:4; 1 Peter 4:12-16).

The next day, the Council interrogated Peter and John. However, a strange reversal of proceedings took place. Although Peter and John were on trial, Annas, Caiaphas and the other members of the Council wound up having to defend their actions. They were powerless in the presence of the cured man. No one could deny the miracle that had happened. To reject the evidence was to be dishonest with the facts. Peter boldly accused the Council of rejecting the Messiah and showed from Psalm 118:22 how their actions placed them outside of salvation. Salvation is found only in the name of Jesus (Acts 4:12).

"Now as they observed the confidence of Peter and John, and understood that they were uneducated and untrained men, they were marveling, and began to recognize them as having been with Jesus" (Acts 4:13). The name in which Peter and John put their trust generated tremendous boldness and gave them the strength they needed to handle such hostile opposition. It was at this point they were recognized as being associates of Jesus.

Such boldness was characteristic of Jesus. After delivering one of His best-known sermons, the people stood perplexed, recognizing that Jesus' teachings were not like those of the scribes and Pharisees. To the contrary, Jesus spoke as one who had authority (Matthew 7:28-29). Never had a man spoken as Jesus (John 7:46). Jesus told His disciples not to worry about what they would say when they found themselves in circumstances like that of Peter and John. When it was necessary, they would know what to say (Matthew 10:19-20). In other words, Jesus would provide what was needed for the moment by the agency of the Holy Spirit. The principle is the same with us. We can obtain the necessary strength to deal with overbearing circumstances in our lives (Philippians 4:13).

Reasons Behind Their Motivation

The Council stood speechless. What were they going to do with Peter and John? They were in a dilemma. If they did nothing, Peter and John would continue to proclaim their message. They had no grounds for bringing charges against them because the man who was healed stood in their midst. Their only option was to attempt to frighten them with a threat. Their threat, however, fell upon deaf ears. Peter and John said they could not and would not stop preaching. Why were these two apostles of Jesus so motivated? They gave two reasons. First, they claimed they had seen Jesus. We must remember that to qualify as an apostle (i.e., one of the twelve), one had to have been with Jesus from His baptism to His ascension (Acts 1:21-22). During this three-year period, the apostles had seen many things. They witnessed first hand the love, patience and the divine nature of Jesus. These experiences could not be easily dismissed. Not many days had passed since the apostles saw Jesus received up into heaven, a fact to which they feverishly testified.

Second, Peter and John had heard the words of Jesus. His sermons, parables and stories were forever stamped upon their immortal souls. Therefore, because they had heard and seen these things, they were not about to deny Him. Jesus had given them too much.

God Hears Our Prayers

After the Council released them, Peter and John did what was only natural – they went to their brethren. Jesus lends His support through His spiritual body, the church. The members of the church function together as a family. Only their own would understand the ordeal Peter and John had experienced. They told the church everything that had happened to them. What an encouragement it must have been for their brethren in the Lord to witness the commitment of these two Christian men.

Once the brethren were all together, they lifted their voices with one accord and prayed to God. Again, this was a natural thing to do. God's people need to pray. Much encouragement is received through prayer. Jesus once stated: "And whatever you ask in My name, that will I do, that the Father may be glorified in the Son. If you ask Me anything in My name, I will do it" (John 14:13-14).

God heard their prayer. To show His approval, God shook the earth beneath them. God assures us by His actions that He hears our prayers today. Peter later wrote that God's ears are attentive to the prayers of His people (1 Peter 3:12). Prayer has earth-shaking power. Prayers offered in the name of Jesus are the most powerful of all.

We Can Change

The blessings found in the name of Jesus are wonderful, but we cannot overlook one more important truth about His name. This particular fact may be difficult for some people to accept. There are *demands* Jesus makes of us, and He has the right to make them if He so chooses. Five reasons are clear in Peter's sermon as to the right that Jesus has to make demands:

• Jesus can make demands because it was through His power the beggar was made whole. After the lame beggar was healed, Peter told the throng this miracle was not done by his own power. No human ability could have cured his physical and spiritual condition.

• Jesus can make demands because He is the Servant of God (i.e., God's Anointed One – the Messiah or King). It was God's divine will to make known His love and grace through Jesus, His Son (John 3:16).

• Jesus can make demands because He is the summation of all the prophetic utterances of the past.

• Jesus can make demands because He is a lawgiver. Moses told the Israelites in Deuteronomy 18 that God was going to raise up a prophet like him who would serve as a lawgiver. Jesus fulfilled this prediction.

• Jesus can make demands because He was raised from the dead. He lives and reigns as Lord. He is described as the "Prince of life" (Acts 3:15). This title reminds us of what Jesus said in John 14:6: "I am the way, and the truth, and the life; no one comes to the Father, but through Me." Before Jesus raised Lazarus from the dead, He said to Martha, "I am the resurrection and the life; he who believes in Me shall live even if he dies" (John 11:25).

Change is the demand Jesus makes of us. Change is the same demand Peter made of those who had gathered on the Day of Pentecost. In fact, the process involved in change is the same. Consider the parallel:

Acts 2:38	Acts 3:19
Repent	Repent
Be baptized	Return
For the forgiveness of sins	That your sins may be wiped away
Receive gift of Holy Spirit	Times of refreshing may come

Peter wasn't preaching anything different; he was only using figures referring to the same demand – change! These two verses reveal clearly what's involved in change.

Think of the Benefits

There are many incentives for us to submit to the demands of Jesus. First, we can be made spiritually whole as the beggar was made physically whole. Second, the sins that have caused a chasm between God and us can be forever removed. Third, God stands ready to give His Holy Spirit to us as a pledge, a type of security deposit, of our inheritance (Ephesians 1:14). And finally, we also have the promise that we shall be glorified when Jesus returns (Acts 3:20; 1 Corinthians 15:42-47).

What happens to people who refuse to submit to the demands of Jesus? Peter says they "shall be utterly destroyed from among the people" (Acts 3:23). Just think, if we will submit, then we will become spiritually whole, gain inward strength, be motivated to serve God, and enjoy the assurance found only in Jesus. Sounds appealing, does it not? What keeps you from repenting and being baptized (Mark 16:16)? Jesus' name is unique. In His name, you can find all you need for spiritual health.

Power Thoughts For Group Discussion

1. This chapter suggests that without Jesus we are like lame beggars. What other figures of speech does Scripture employ to describe our spiritual condition without God? (See Isaiah 1:5-6, 18.)

2. How does Jesus cure spiritual diseases? What kind of help does He offer that's different from what others may provide?

3. Paul said, "And indeed, all who desire to live godly in Christ Jesus will be persecuted" (2 Timothy 3:12). Discuss the various ways in which Christians might be persecuted today. Has the church been effective in preparing Christians for persecution?

4. Why do many today look with disfavor upon the church? How did Peter and John view the church?

5. What rewards will be given to those who have submitted themselves to Jesus? Will these rewards be enjoyed only in the future, or are there any present benefits?

Chapter 5

The Courage to Be Genuine
Acts 5:1-11

"I am looking for an honest man."
Diogenes

People are not always what they appear to be. Alan Loy McGinnis'
book, *The Friendship Factor*, has a chapter titled, "The Art of Self-
Disclosure," in which he indicates that people are attracted to genuine
people. Genuineness is attractive because it projects a certain degree of
transparency. People who are transparent are comfortable and encouraging to be around. It makes sense to me. The more I have opened up to
others, the closer my relationships have become. This principle is cru-
cial if lasting and strong relationships are to be cultivated and enjoyed.

Facing Our Facades

The problem is people generally have a tendency to put up facades.
People want to be liked by other people. "But if people really knew
me," some of us think, "they would reject me." Just the opposite is true.
People gravitate to those who are honest and sincere.

The word "sincere" comes from a Latin word meaning "without
wax." Its etymology originates with the ancient street vendor who sold
clay figurines. Often venders, upon discovering defects in the clay fig-
urine, covered them up by mixing clay residue with wax and applying

the mixture to the product. Later in the customer's home after the wax had dried, the defect would be exposed. Because consumers were being jilted, such a practice hurt the trade. Therefore, other vendors began to advertise their product as *sine cera*, meaning "without wax."

The most scathing rebuke Jesus ever gave was against the hypocrisy of the scribes and Pharisees. On the surface, they appeared to be genuinely committed to God, but underneath in their hearts, they were filled with all kinds of corruption (Matthew 23). Jesus could see right through their religious veneer and said they would be getting a reward, but not the kind they had in mind.

God Sees the Heart

God knows our hearts. He knows who we really are. It's futile to try to outwit Him, for everyone is laid bare before His eyes (Hebrews 4:13). "Half of the misery in the world," wrote George MacDonald, "comes from trying to look, instead of trying to be, what one is not." I'm reminded of how true the saying by Abraham Lincoln really is: "You can fool some of the people all of the time, and all of the people some of the time, but you cannot fool all of the people all of the time." More often than not, people wise up and come to recognize the masquerade. What religion needs is more genuine people.

Acts 4:32 begins a tragic story about two first-century Christians, Ananias and Sapphira. Two different groups of Christians are contrasted in this narrative. One group is genuine; the other is not. This story, no doubt, is preserved in Scripture by the Holy Spirit to impress us with God's demand for service rendered from pure motives.

A Selfless Community

The sacrificial attitude of first-century Christians overflowed with generosity. Their actions were predictable. They simply followed in the footsteps of their Savior, Jesus Christ.

Jesus is a selfless leader. In a world where there is a constant battle for the top spot, the teachings of Jesus can be difficult to grasp. The mother of James and John wanted what every mother wants for her children – the best. She came to Jesus and requested that her sons be placed on His right and on His left in the kingdom. This request didn't set too well with the other disciples because they also coveted positions of distinction. As a result, an argument broke out among the disciples about who was the greatest among them. Jesus interrupted and explained to them how things were different in His kingdom (Matthew 20:20-28).

Power Plays

The people of the world love authority. They love to be in positions where they can "lord" over others. In contrast, the top spot in God's kingdom is at the bottom. Jesus said, "[W]hoever wishes to become great among you shall be your servant; and whoever wishes to be first among you shall be your slave" (Matthew 20:26-27). Jesus then revealed the premise of His teaching: "[J]ust as the Son of Man did not come to be served, but to serve, and to give His life a ransom for many" (v. 28). If anyone could glory in his high position, it could have been Jesus, but He didn't.

On another occasion, when Jesus was eating with His disciples in the upper room, He arose while His disciples were reclined at the table, poured water into a basin, took a towel, and began to wash their feet. It was customary for a house servant to wash the guests' feet as they entered the house. No such servant was present. It would have been beneath the dignity of the disciples to assume such a lowly position, but it wasn't beneath Jesus to do so. After He sat down, Jesus said: "You call Me Teacher and Lord; and you are right, for so I am. If I then, the Lord and the Teacher, washed your feet, you also ought to wash one another's feet. For I gave you an example that you also should do as I did to you" (John 13:13-15).

The actions of Jesus were consistent with Paul's appraisal of Him: "Have this attitude in yourselves which was also in Christ Jesus, who, although He existed in the form of God, did not regard equality with God a thing to be grasped, but emptied Himself, taking the form of a bond-servant, and being made in the likeness of men. And being found in appearance as a man, He humbled Himself by becoming obedient to the point of death, even death on a cross" (Philippians 2:5-8). Paul exhorts us to get our thinking straight by having this same attitude of humility.

A Caring Church

The church is the product of selflessness. There's not a better expression of selflessness than Christ's voluntary death for our sins. The church for which He died became the bountiful fruit of His selfless act (Acts 20:28). No wonder the members of the Jerusalem church were so generous toward one another (Acts 2:44-45; 4:32-37). Generosity flows naturally when we follow Jesus. The motivating factor behind their generosity wasn't fame or fortune. Luke said they were believers, and that made all the difference in the world. What they believed in is told in Acts 4:33: "And with great power the apostles were giving witness to the resurrection of the Lord Jesus, and abundant grace was upon them."

The truthfulness of the resurrection had brought the disciples together in such a way that Luke wrote they were of "one heart and soul" (Acts 4:32). They were linked together. This common bond motivated them to share their possessions with others, so no one among them would be in need. The selfless life is truly the most powerful of all.

The Beauty of Barnabas

Of all the possibilities to choose from, Luke holds before us Barnabas as a prime example of selfless living. Barnabas, of course, may have been chosen because of the key role he played in the church (Acts 9:27; 11:22, 30; 12:25; 13:1-2, 7; 1 Corinthians 9:6; Galatians 2:1, 9, 13; Colossians 4:10). We are told Barnabas' name means "son of encouragement."

It's important to realize a ministry of encouragement, in which Barnabas excelled, is only possible when people are genuine. When he sold a tract of land, Barnabas didn't hold anything back. He brought all the proceeds to the apostles and laid it at their feet. Barnabas' example must surely have encouraged the church. Only selfless people can take what they have and give it to another without expecting anything in return. The action of Barnabas was a natural outgrowth of his Christianity.

A Selfish Couple

In contrast to Jesus, the church and Barnabas were the attitudes of Ananias and Sapphira. Without being too judgmental, could we not say that Ananias and Sapphira were overlaid with Christian veneer? They were associated with the community of believers, but somehow it was secondary to their agenda. They allowed self instead of Christ to control them. When that happens, Christianity is inclined to be less genuine.

Twice it is emphasized that Ananias kept back some of the money they had been given for the field (Acts 5:2-3). Both Ananias and Sapphira were unwilling to let go of what they had. It wasn't wrong for them to keep a portion of the proceeds of their property. What they decided to do with the money was under their control. Their error was in giving the appearance they had given all the money. Tragically, some people in the church are filled with the same deceitful spirit as Ananias and Sapphira. People who want all the benefits and blessings Christianity offers, but who are unwilling to pay the price, are "Christians" in the likeness of Ananias and Sapphira.

Watch Out for These

What factors led to the spiritual demise of these two? It could have been greed. Many souls have fallen prey to the vice of greed. During the days of Malachi, the Israelites were holding back. God accused them of robbing Him. He exhorted them to bring the "whole tithe into the storehouse" (Malachi 3:8-12). The Israelites had more to gain by giving and much more to lose by keeping.

Ananias and Sapphira may have coveted the praise of their peers. Barnabas received a lot of recognition and praise for what he had done. Ananias and Sapphira could have lusted for the same thing, but were reluctant to make the same sacrifice.

The actions of Ananias and Sapphira illustrate the truth contained in James 1:13-15:

> Let no one say when he is tempted, "I am being tempted by God"; for God cannot be tempted by evil, and He Himself does not tempt anyone. But each one is tempted when he is carried away and enticed by his own lust. Then when lust has conceived, it gives birth to sin; and when sin is accomplished, it brings forth death.

Satan took advantage of their selfishness and was able to entice them to do wrong. Peter said to them that they had allowed Satan to fill their hearts. They had given themselves over to their lusts by following through with their plan. Consequently, both of them were paid their wages – death (Romans 6:23). Ananias and Sapphira's dreadful mistake was imagining they could use religion as a cloak for personal gain (James 4:3; 1 Peter 2:16). "For whoever wishes to save his life shall lose it; but whoever loses his life for My sake shall find it" (Matthew 16:25).

A Serious Crime

Some people may accuse God of dealing too harshly with Ananias and Sapphira. However, how they died is not nearly as important as why they died.

God's actions are just and appropriate. Ananias and Sapphira committed a serious crime. They lied to the Holy Spirit and to God, and they put the Spirit of the Lord to the test. Their actions brought God's character and word into disrepute. If God had not dealt with this sin immediately, countless people would have thought Him to be a pushover. God cannot be deceived. Read Hebrews 4:12-13:

> For the word of God is living and active and sharper than any two-edged sword, and piercing as far as the division of soul and spirit, of both joints and marrow, and able to judge the thoughts and intentions of the heart. And there is no creature hidden from His sight, but all things are open and laid bare to the eyes of Him with whom we have to do.

Ananias and Sapphira also committed a serious crime against the church. They were dishonest with their brethren, and many other Christians could have been led astray by the error. Paul rebuked the church in Corinth for not dealing with the man in their midst who was involved in an immoral relationship (1 Corinthians 5). He warned them that the purity of the church was going to be destroyed – "a little leaven leavens the whole lump of dough" (v. 6). By their actions, Ananias and Sapphira were encouraging others to sin.

Finally, Ananias and Sapphira committed a terrible crime against themselves. Sin ultimately hurts the sinner. The gospel is a message for those who are hurting themselves.

A story is told about a poor carpenter who was hired by a man to build a house. After the agreement was made, the man went on a trip. The carpenter decided to take advantage of his employer's absence, and so he used shoddy material in the house's construction and took shortcuts in places that couldn't be seen. The house was finished and appeared to be a very beautiful and well-constructed home. The owner finally returned and was impressed with the house's appearance. "You did a fine job," the owner said. Then he gave the deed of the property and the key to the poor carpenter and said, "It's yours!" The poor carpenter grieved because he had cheated himself.

Who Is in Control?

The name Ananias means "the Lord is gracious," and Sapphira means "beautiful." Ironically, their names told a far different story than their lives. Are we putting up facades? Christ-ruled people tend to be selfless and give all they have to the task. On the other hand, self-ruled people are more likely to be selfish and hold back from doing what could potentially bless their lives. Are we overlaid with Christian veneer? Are we holding back? If we are, then we're no better than Ananias and Sapphira. If we're going to be Christians, then let's not play games with our Christianity. God won't play. In her book *God Is No Fool*, Lois A. Cheney reminds us why God is not a pushover.

They say that God has infinite patience,
And that is a great comfort.

They say God is always there,
And that is a deep satisfaction.

They say that God will always take you back,
And I get lazy in that certitude.

They say that God never gives up,
And I count on that.

They say you can go away for years and years,
And he'll be there, waiting, when you come back.

They say you can make mistake after mistake,
And God will always forgive and forget.

They say lots of things,
These people who never read the Old Testament.

There comes a time,
A definite, for sure time,
When God turns around.

I don't believe God shed his skin
When Christ brought in the New Testament;
Christ showed us a new side of God,
And it is truly wonderful.

But he didn't change God.
God remains forever and ever
And that God
is
no
fool (55-56).

Power Thoughts for Group Discussion

1. What factors in our world pressure people to appear to be what they're not? How does such pressure affect a person inwardly?

2. Can a selfless Christian really survive in a selfish world?

3. The church has been described by some as consisting of volunteers. How then do you get a body of volunteers to give of their time, money and talents to the work of the church?

4. How do you feel about the death of Ananias and Sapphira? How would you justify God's grace, mercy and love in view of such a tragedy?

5. In what ways can a person be injured by committing sin? Why do people keep on sinning if they know it will ultimately harm them?

Chapter 6

The Courage to See

Acts 5:17-32

"In a dark time, the eye begins to see."
Theodore Roethke

I was a stagehand once in a musical production and was overwhelmed by the amount of activity going on behind the curtains. After each act, props were removed and set up again, actors changed apparel and secured their positions, and it all transpired in a matter of seconds! No one knew how hard I was working behind those curtains. From the perspective of the audience, the musical was a smooth-flowing and awe-inspiring production. Behind the scenes, however, was a different story.

It's fascinating to watch how movies are made. The movie *Star Wars* brought about a proliferation of science fiction movies many years ago. The special effects were enthralling. Who would have thought those spaceships and planets were nothing more than miniature models? They looked so big and real on the screen. When we enjoy those delightful animated movies, we don't think about the thousands of individual drawings that went into their production. We would also be astonished if we caught a glimpse of what is behind the scenes in the world.

Throughout history, God has been working behind the scenes to carry out His will. This divine activity is often referred to as God's providence. Read God's promise in Romans 8:28. Acts 5:12-42 is a demonstration of how He works in our world. Our purpose in what follows will be to analyze the activity of God in the lives of the apostles, other people (both favorable and not so favorable to Christianity), and in our lives. If we come to accept all that is implied in this section of Scripture, we will, with renewed vigor, forge uncompromisingly forward in our Christian walk.

God's Ambassadors

God did the unbelievable while working through His apostles. Remember, the apostles were the special leaders of the early church. Jesus told them they would be empowered by the Holy Spirit to be witnesses of His resurrection (Acts 1:5-8). They shared an intimate relationship with Him for about three years – from the time He was baptized until the time He was received into heaven. Upon the foundation of the apostles' teachings, the church (superstructure) was erected (Ephesians 2:20). Through the apostles and the preservation of their writings, the church was edified and continues to be enriched today (4:11-13).

According to Acts 2:4, the apostles received the miraculous indwelling of the Holy Spirit: "And they were all filled with the Holy Spirit and began to speak with other tongues, as the Spirit was giving them utterance." This unique indwelling of the Holy Spirit enabled them to perform miracles. Their miracles indicated that God was operating in and through them (Hebrews 2:1-4).

These miracles were unexplainable phenomena. Even the words selected by Luke to describe them emphasize their supernatural origin. "Miracles," "signs" and "wonders" were special words underscoring supernatural activity. The word "miracle" revealed that certain phenomena were not of the natural realm for the simple reason that they could not be reproduced by any natural means (see Acts 8:13 for an illustration). The nature of the word "sign" pointed beyond itself; it was a token or indication of something greater. The word "wonder" captured the emotion generated in others who, after witnessing something mysterious, strange or spectacular, marveled at such a sight (4:16, 22, 30). All three of these words were used in Peter's sermon recorded in Acts 2:22 as they related to the ministry of Jesus.

The Purpose of Miracles

At this point it may be beneficial to pause and note the purpose of miracles. Miracles basically had a threefold function.

(1) Miracles were God's way of showing compassion for those who had physical and/or mental needs. God showed His concern for the hurts of others by working through Jesus and the apostles to heal those who were sick (Matthew 4:23-25; Acts 5:15-16).

(2) Miracles confirmed the credentials of the people performing them. The apostles were held in high esteem, no doubt, because they were no ordinary men. They were the messengers of God, empowered by Him to perform miracles, signs and wonders.

(3) Miracles served as a preparatory device to condition people for the reception of a spiritual truth. According to John 6, Jesus showed heavenly compassion when He fed more than 5,000 hungry people (function #1 above). Feeding this great multitude from five barley loaves and two fish confirmed His claim to be divine (function #2). However, the foregoing event led up to the spiritual truth that Jesus was the "bread of life" (function #3).

Nothing Too Difficult for God

God not only did the unbelievable, but He also accomplished the impossible. The success of the apostles filled the elite membership of the Jewish Council with rage. They arrested the apostles and put them in jail; but even in jail, God was with His special ambassadors. Although the jail was locked securely and guards were stationed at the doors, it was not secure enough to keep God out. God sent His angel during the night to open the gates of the jail and rescue the apostles without anyone ever knowing about it. What appeared to be an impossible task was no contest for God. Jeremiah knew about God's amazing power when he wrote in Jeremiah 32:17-27: "Ah Lord God! Behold, Thou hast made the heavens and the earth by Thy great power and by Thine outstretched arm! Nothing is too difficult for Thee ... . 'Behold, I am the Lord, the God of all flesh; is anything too difficult for Me?' "

God freely breaks the barriers of impossibilities. Examples from the past serve as vivid reminders of God's power. He demonstrated His power when He brought the Israelites out of Egyptian captivity. He convinced Elisha's servant of His power when He delivered the prophet from a seemingly hopeless situation (2 Kings 6:8-19). Now God was going to confound the Jewish authorities by rescuing the apostles from jail. After the jailbreak, God commanded the apostles to go and preach. Their message was too important to be kept locked up.

With such a spectacular rescue, the apostles had courage to speak again to the people in the temple and even the gall to preach to the Council! Peter spoke forthrightly, saying, "The God of our fathers raised up Jesus whom you had put to death by hanging Him on a cross" (Acts 5:30). Who's on trial here, anyway? The apostles were, of course, but the Jewish Council also stood before the tribunal of God. Naturally, the Council didn't like what was happening, so they intended to murder the apostles. Don't forget that God was still around.

Unexpected Allies

Jesus gives the promise of His presence to all His disciples as they carry out His Great Commission. He said in Matthew 28:20: "and lo, I am with you always, even to the end of the age." One way we enjoy the presence of God is by knowing He often works on our behalf by employing others.

When the religious leaders laid hands on the apostles, they did so without violence. The common people gladly heard the message of the gospel, but the religious leaders wanted to take violent actions against the apostles. Parenthetically, Luke tells why the apostles were taken without violence: "for they were afraid of the people, lest they should be stoned" (Acts 5:26). Could God be behind the calm way in which the apostles were arrested? It is interesting to think God may have employed the people as a type of buffer around them.

When dealing with God's people, the fear of the people often leads those who oppose the preaching and teaching of the gospel down a more congenial path. A good friend of mine related an incident that happened while he was doing missionary work in Sri Lanka. He had converted a Buddhist, and this newly converted man was in danger of losing his life. The Buddhist priest found out where this man lived and sent a delegation to take him. Upon arrival at the Christian's residence, the Buddhists were surprised to find that Muslims, with their swords drawn, had formed a bastion around the Christian man. In fear and frustration, the Buddhists left. This Christian was such a respectable man even people of other religious faiths shielded him from violence. We may not be able to explain how He does it, but we can be certain that God carries out His will even if it means operating through others to achieve it.

The Council wanted to exterminate the apostles. The apostles, however, found an unexpected defender among them. Gamaliel was a Pharisee and an esteemed teacher of the Law. He ordered the removal of the apostles from the meeting. He then proceeded to caution the other members of the Council to avoid extreme and violent actions against the apostles. He proposed if these men were not of God then their movement would eventually dissipate. On the other hand, he advised, if this movement was of God "you will not be able to overthrow them; or else you may even be found fighting against God." Were the actions of Gamaliel providential? Could it be that God was working through Gamaliel on behalf of the apostles?

In John 7:50-52 a Pharisee named Nicodemus stood up in defense of Jesus – a courageous thing to do. Later, John records how Nicodemus participated in the burial of Jesus by donating more than 100 pounds of spices (19:39-40). Nicodemus, like Gamaliel, was another unexpected ally.

Not only does God use those who may be sympathetic to His cause to carry out His will, He also will employ those who are hostile toward us for His purposes. Regarding Pharaoh, Paul wrote, "For the Scripture says to Pharaoh, 'For this very purpose I raised you up, to demonstrate My power in you, and that My name might be proclaimed throughout the whole earth' " (Romans 9:17). God employed the hostile attitude of the Jews to carry out His plan of redemption in Jesus Christ. Those who chanted, "Crucify Him, crucify Him," were oblivious to the fact that they were actually carrying out God's design for the redemption of humanity. Even the angry Saul of Tarsus was unaware that God had plans for him. Saul's persecution served as a catalyst to promote the evangelistic efforts of the church beyond the land of Judea (Acts 7:58; 8:4; cf. 1:8). God can and will work through others to achieve His purposes.

The tragedy in all of this is that those choosing to fight against God will be overthrown. Psalm 2:1-6 is a plea for humanity to lay down its rebellion and worship the Lord. The psalmist cautioned:

Why are the nations in an uproar, And the peoples devising a vain thing? The kings of the earth take their stand, And the rulers take counsel together Against the Lord and against His Anointed: "Let us tear their fetters apart, And cast away their cords from us!" He who sits in the heavens laughs, The Lord scoffs at them. Then He will speak to them in His anger And terrify them in His fury: But as for Me, I have installed My King Upon Zion, My holy mountain.

Let it be known that no puny human being will be able to overthrow the will of God; His word abides forever (1 Peter 1:25; Isaiah 55:11).

A Passionate Faith

Now if God was with the apostles and if He also worked out impossible circumstances for their good and the good of His cause, shouldn't we be more resolute to be about our heavenly Father's business? After all, if God is for us who can be against us (Romans 8:31)? God also helps us behind the scenes.

The Christians of the first century possessed two overwhelming passions. First, their gratitude for all God had done for them caused them to feel it was a privilege to serve Him. The Jewish Council decided to release the apostles, but before they did, they flogged them and ordered them not to preach anymore in the name of Jesus Christ. The beatings and the threats went unheeded. The apostles believed it was an honor to suffer for Christ. Look at what Jesus had suffered for them (1 Peter 2:21-25). In fact, they went from the presence of the Council rejoicing! "[B]ut if anyone suffers as a Christian, let him not feel ashamed, but in that name let him glorify God" (4:16).

The second gripping passion of first-century Christians was their belief that serving God was their profession. Every Christian may have an occupation, but every Christian has only one profession. Paul teaches that when we become Christians we are given the ministry (or profession) of reconciliation (2 Corinthians 5:18). Our occupation may be in the field of medical science, accounting, business management, athletics, education or homemaking; however, our profession is Christianity. Such was the attitude of the early Christians; their religion was an everyday affair and an every place endeavor (Acts 2:42). Thus, Paul encourages us to "be steadfast, immovable, always abounding in the work of the Lord" (1 Corinthians 15:58). And why shouldn't we, if we know that God is working behind the curtains upon the stage of life?

Fanatics for Christ

The apostles were committed to their task. Peter and John said earlier when threatened, "We cannot stop speaking what we have seen and heard." Peter and the other apostles boldly answered the Council, "We must obey God rather than men" (Acts 5:29), and they continued to keep right on "preaching Jesus as the Christ" (v. 42). Were they fanatics? Certainly they were! Any believer will appear to unbelievers as fanatical. Knowing that Jesus lives and that God is at work behind the scenes energizes a Christian's commitment.

I heard a story about a little girl who took a long trip on a train. Her destination required that the train pass over several rivers. As the train approached each river, the little girl would clutch her fists in fear, wondering how the train would be able to cross the water. Then, suddenly, a bridge would appear, and the train would cross over safely. After this happened several times, the little girl, finally relieved, leaned back and took a deep breath. "Somebody has put bridges for us all the way!" she said with confidence. Perhaps, in a real sense, this little girl verbalizes the confidence all Christians should have in the providential workings of God.

Power Thoughts for Group Discussion

1. Discuss the purpose of miracles in light of Hebrews 1:1-4. Make a list of at least 10 miracles performed by Jesus and note beside each its purpose.

2. How would you explain the providence of God? Does the providence of God necessarily assume miraculous activity?

3. What other examples can you give illustrating how God has worked through non-Christians on behalf of His people.

4. How is it possible for a Christian to rejoice while suffering? What unique perspective does a Christian bring to such a situation?

5. If you viewed Christianity as your number one profession, what changes would you make in your life?

Chapter 7

The Courage to Include

"Our military forces are one team – in the game to win
regardless of who carries the ball."
Gen. Omar N. Bradley

To increase productivity and promote pride within the company, many companies today have made their employees part owners. The idea is logical – people tend to care for the things they own. People also like to be a part of something bigger than themselves. One preacher told about a humorous thing that happened while he was preaching in Waycross, Ga.:

> When I was a local minister in Waycross, Ga., I coached pee-wee football. Those were the earth-shattering days of "Quarterman Owls" and the "William Heights Indians." Although there were other teams in the league, we were the ones that traditionally fought it out for the title. Although we lost the title that year, we managed to place a number of players on the all-star team. This was the one special game (played under the lights) that attracted some 200 fans (which was about 180 more than our day games).

> Two things happened during the game that are uniquely human. As the clock wound down to less than a minute, the

bench was cleared, and one youngster (extremely small for his age) was put in the right tackle spot. He had been selected because of his great spirit for the game and his loyalty to the team. As the signals were called and the line was set, he reached for a handful of dirt and spread it on his jersey. After a play or two the gun sounded and the game was over. As the young gladiator came to the sidelines, mud on his jersey, he excitedly proclaimed, "I didn't make any tackles, but I jumped on the pile twice!"

This young boy may not have had all the talent in the world, but he expressed a universal sentiment. People want to play a unique role in the game of life.

One Body, Many Members

Although not necessarily parallel, the church is somewhat the same. One of the blessings gained from being a member of the church is the awareness that we are vital components of Christ's spiritual body. Because Christ's body on earth is composed of individuals, it follows that individuals like ourselves would take a keen interest in its spiritual health (1 Corinthians 12). It should be natural for us as members of the church to be acutely aware of those things that would build up or destroy the body. Many church members, however, never seem to capture the vision that they are vital links to the success or failure of the local church.

The first-century church overcame many obstacles. It survived the hostile attacks of the Jewish Council (Acts 4:3-4; 5:12-42). It also survived Satan's attempt to destroy the church from within (5:1-11). As more and more people come to know Jesus and are added to His church, the question remains whether the church will continue to maintain a unified spirit. The account in Acts 6:1-7 served as a critical test.

Differences Can Divide

The church is composed of people, and when people are brought together we can expect problems. A fuss arose between two distinct groups in the early church – those of native Hebrew background and those of a Greek background. The Day of Pentecost brought many non-Palestinian Jews to Jerusalem. These Jews, although of one kindred with those of the land of Palestine, were distinctively different. They had a Greek flavor to them in their speech and in their lifestyles, so much so that they were almost more than the native Palestinian Jew could bear.

When Peter preached the gospel on the eventful Day of Pentecost, multitudes of both Hellenistic (Greek speaking) and native Hebrew Jews responded and became Christians. From that day forward, the church cared for the welfare of each member to such an extent that many of the early Christians made personal sacrifices to help (Acts 4:32-37). The Jerusalem church even established a daily ministry of benevolence. However, petty grievances between the two groups of Jewish Christians slowly surfaced.

The Greek-speaking disciples thought their widows were being overlooked in the daily distribution of food. Was this neglect an intentional oversight? Maybe, maybe not, but it was a real problem nonetheless. The uniting of these two culturally different groups created problems for the church. Such problems, however, should have been expected from the beginning.

The church in Corinth also had its problems with differing personalities. Groups of Christians had gravitated to certain preachers who appealed to them, and instead of enjoying a harmonious fellowship, these groups viewed each other as rivals. No wonder Paul commanded them to be united in the same mind and in the same judgment (1 Corinthians 1:10). Certainly, their attitudes were not very Christian.

When Paul wrote the letter to the Philippians, he pleaded with two women, Euodia and Syntyche, to live in harmony with one another (Philippians 4:2). Evidently a severe problem existed between these women. What the problem was is untold. Whatever the problem may have been, the dispute confirmed the obvious – in any gathering of people, there will always be problems.

Because problems naturally arise among people of different backgrounds, it is essential that each member of the church become involved in the solution-making process. The necessity of such involvement is made vividly clear when Paul stated that "there should be no division in the body, but that the members should have the same care for one another" (1 Corinthians 12:25). The church needs more workers and fewer whiners.

The possible oversight of some in the Jerusalem church may very well have been the result of complacency more than anything else. The church must not neglect her people. It's necessary for all to get involved because every member is important to Jesus (Acts 20:28).

Getting Involved

When the problem reached the ears of the apostles, they called the congregation together. The church needed to get its priorities in order. As important as the daily ministry of benevolence was, it was not the most important priority. According to Acts 6:4, the church has three important tasks: prayer, proclamation and provision. But are these equal in their importance? The apostles didn't think so.

The first task at the top of the list was prayer. As stated previously, the early church was a praying community. It was important for the apostles to spend time in prayer. James even wrote that if any lacked wisdom, he could ask for it in prayer and God would liberally bestow it (James 1:5).

The second task on the list of priorities was proclaiming the Word. Interestingly, the apostles informed the congregation that they were involved in a daily ministry of serving the Word of God. The Word of God is of such importance that without its proclamation no one can be saved (Acts 4:12; James 1:21).

The last item on the list was providing for the needs of church members. Social concerns must be handled; however, the church is not simply a social project. When churches give most of their attention to the social aspects of life, they neglect those essential elements that promote growth and stability – namely, prayer and proclamation.

Clearly, the apostles were key players in the daily ministry of benevolence. When funds were received from the sale of property or possessions, they were brought to Jerusalem and laid at the apostles' feet (Acts 4:35, 37; 5:2). They would then see to it that the funds were distributed to the appropriate place. This procedure, no doubt, continued to be followed on a daily basis. It was as if the church was relying upon the apostles for everything, even in those things members could do for themselves. Tragically, if their reliance upon the apostles continued much longer, there was the real possibility that the apostles would begin to neglect their primary obligation to proclaim Christ to all the world (1:8).

There's always a tendency to allow a few to do the work of the many. Preachers are expected to be men of many talents. They are usually required to be involved in every work of the church. But what the church doesn't realize is that they are forcing the preacher to neglect the very thing he was called to do – preach the Word!

The church shouldn't be a community in which a few do the work for the many. On the contrary, each member works in conjunction with other members. There is work for all to do. The problem recorded in Acts 6:1 should never have reached the ears of the apostles. Did not these two groups of Christian Jews have enough maturity to seek a solution together? What was the real problem? Indifference. The church lacked involvement.

Paul urges Christians to use the abilities God has endowed them for the betterment of the church. He wrote in Romans 12:4-8:

> For just as we have many members in one body and all the members do not have the same function, so we, who are many, are one body in Christ, and individually members of one another. And since we have gifts that differ according to the grace given to us, let each exercise them accordingly: if prophecy, according to proportion of his faith; if service, in his serving; or he who teaches, in his teaching; or he who exhorts, in his exhortation; he who gives, with liberality; he who leads, with diligence; he who shows mercy, with cheerfulness.

In other words, let's do our part! When a few within the spiritual body of Christ struggle to take up the slack of the uninvolved, they may lose their effectiveness in their most qualified areas. After the apostles established the top priorities, they were now ready to include others in the solution to the problem.

Everyone Is Included

Before the situation got too far out of hand, the apostles immediately guided the congregation through the problem-solving process. This process involved three important steps:

(1) Tap into the right resource. The apostles said to "select from among you, brethren, seven men" (Acts 6:3). It's amazing how churches are oblivious to the fact that they are their own best resource for seeking solutions to their problems. The church is filled with multi-talented people. We must include them. When leaders turn to the members of the church, they are tapping into the best resource available. The church in Jerusalem was unaware that she had the resources to solve the problem created by the daily distribution of food.

Paul expressed bewilderment when he learned some brethren in the church at Corinth were taking one another to the courts of unbelievers to settle their disputes. He wrote in 1 Corinthians 6:5: "I say this to your shame. Is it so, that there is not among you one wise man who will be able to decide between his brethren?" Why weren't the brethren in the church at Corinth tapping into their own rich resources?

Paul also encouraged the involvement of the brethren in the church at Philippi to help solve the problems between Euodia and Syntyche. He specifically referred to a man whom he identified as a "true comrade" and a man named Clement. These two, together with the rest of the brethren, needed to help these women overcome their problems (Philippians 4:2-3). How sad it is when Christians stand by and watch the church tear itself apart. "All that is necessary for evil to triumph," said Edmund Burke, "is that good men do nothing." Therefore, the first step in the problem-solving process was to turn to the best resource available – the church.

(2) Temperament must match the responsibility. The apostles said the seven men to be selected were to be "of good reputation, full of the Spirit and of wisdom" (Acts 6:3). The situation called for men of special temperaments or qualities. They were to be above reproach, men of integrity.

The best test to determine the moral makeup of an individual is to consider his reputation. What kind of life does he lead? Naturally, this first quality gave way to the second. He was to be "full of the Spirit" (Acts 6:3). It's possible the apostles were referring to some type of miraculous manifestation of the Holy Spirit found in the lives of some of the church members. Philip, who was one of the seven selected, had such evidence (v. 5; 8:4-8). However, to possess the Holy Spirit is not always synonymous with the possession of miraculous powers. The Spirit-filled life consists of such things as love, joy, peace, patience, kindness, goodness, faithfulness, gentleness and self-control (Galatians 5:22-23).

These men were also to have wisdom. Without wisdom, the delicate problem between the Hellenistic and the Hebrew Christians could develop into a solid line of division. Therefore, the second step in the problem-solving process was to match the temperament with the responsibility.

(3) Entrust the task. The final step taken to reach a solution to the widow problem involved the entrustment of the task given to the seven men selected by the church. These men were in charge of and responsible for making sure the dispute was settled. The seven were "brought before the apostles; and after praying, they laid their hands on them" (Acts 6:13). The action of laying on of hands was a symbolic act expressing a charge or entrustment. Before Paul left on his first mission tour with Barnabas, the church in Antioch fasted and prayed and then laid their hands on them (13:3). The church was basically saying, "May the Lord be with you as you fulfill His mission."

Along with the entrustment of the task also comes the responsibility of seeing it to completion. Success or failure was placed upon the shoulders of those selected. The position, indeed, was one of honor, but it also carried with it a high degree of accountability. This third step in the problem-solving process was perhaps the most challenging. Without its implementation, there could be no solution to the problem.

Seeking Solutions

Was the problem in Acts 6:1-7 merely a simple oversight of the need of the Grecian widows, or was the real problem one of inclusion? Were the members of the church taking an active part? There's a story about a man who attempted to master the art of swimming. He bought an instructional manual and day after day he would lie beside the pool and practice all the strokes. One day while walking around the pool, he got too close to the edge and fell in. If someone hadn't jumped in and pulled him to safety the man would have drowned! There is a big difference between practicing the art of swimming beside the water and actually swimming in the water. Next time, when problems arise in the church, make sure you get involved and help seek a solution.

Power Thoughts for Group Discussion

1. In his book *How Does America Hear the Gospel*, William A. Dyrness wrote: "Individualism in our modern sense of self-sufficiency seems more closely related to the attempt of Adam and Eve to be their own gods. The self-realizing, self-defining individual too often becomes a barrier to hearing the cries of his neighbor or obeying the voice of God" (103).

   How has our nation's emphasis upon individualism affected how we relate to one another as a community of believers?

2. How does your congregation normally handle problems when they arise?

3. It has been said that in the church 20 percent of the people do 80 percent of the work. What are the underlying factors promoting such an imbalance? Should all the blame go toward the 80 percent? Do the 20 percent bear any responsibility for the imbalance?

4. How could the church better use the talents of her members?

5. "If you want something done right, you've got to do it yourself." How has this adage impacted the church? What is implied by this statement?

Chapter 8

The Courage to Die

Acts 7:51-60

"If we must die, O let us nobly die."
Claude McKay

Polycarp, a Christian man, was burned at the stake in A.D. 155. Tradition tells us he learned about Jesus from the aged apostle John. After being told to worship Caesar and to denounce Christ, he replied, "Eighty and six years have I served him, and he never did me wrong; and how can I now blaspheme my King that has saved me?" Threatened again with fire, he exclaimed, "You threaten fire that burns for a moment and is soon extinguished, for you know nothing of the judgment to come, and the fire of eternal punishment reserved for the wicked. But why do you delay? Bring what you wish" (Eusebius, *Ecclesiastical History*, IV, XV, 146). Polycarp's commitment to Jesus cost him his life.

No Cowards in This Crowd

I've always admired the dedication of people in the past who have been willing to die for their faith. When Nebuchadnezzar threatened Shadrach, Meshach and Abednego with death in the furnace of fire if they did not bow to the idol made of gold, these three young Jews courageously refused (Daniel 3). Many others, likewise, have shown a similar spirit. Hebrews 11:32-38 briefly summarizes, in striking language, the dedication of some of God's faithful followers:

> And what more shall I say? For time will fail me if I tell of Gideon, Barak, Samson, Jephthah, of David and Samuel and the prophets, who by faith conquered kingdoms, performed acts of righteousness, obtained promises, shut the mouths of lions, quenched the power of fire, escaped the edge of the sword, from weakness were made strong, became mighty in war, put foreign armies to flight. Women received back their dead by resurrection; and others were tortured, not accepting their release, in order that they might obtain a better resurrection; and others experienced mockings and scourgings, yes, also chains and imprisonment. They were stoned, they were sawn in two, they were tempted, they were put to death with a sword; they went about in sheepskins, in goatskins, being destitute, afflicted, ill-treated (men of whom the world was not worthy), wandering in deserts and mountains and caves and holes in the ground.

The Jewish Council persecuted Peter and John. According to Acts 4:1-21, the Council released them after issuing stern threats for them not to speak anymore about Jesus. The apostles ignored their threats and continued to proclaim the gospel of Jesus Christ while enjoying a good reception by the general population. In a jealous rage, the Jewish leaders began a second wave of persecution. This time they put all the apostles in jail, beat them, and threatened them further (Acts 5:17-40). "Remember the word that I said to you," Jesus once told His disciples, " 'A slave is not greater than his master.' If they persecuted Me, they will also persecute you" (John 15:20).

Too Close to Home

In Acts 7, another wave of persecution begins. This one, however, is not against the apostles, but against a Christian man named Stephen. Now ordinary members of the church are being abused for their faith. How pertinent then is the life and faith of Stephen to our lives? He was simply a Christian like us. Yet, there was something extraordinary about him.

Stephen played such an important role in the growth of the church that the contributions he made as well as his death are stamped upon the immortal pages of the Bible for all to read. His death is even recorded before the death of an apostle (Acts 12:1-2). Great leaders, not ordinary citizens, are usually honored and celebrated. In the kingdom of God, however, the last are first, and the small are great.

Now we are ready to look into the mind of Stephen to uncover those qualities motivating his dedication to Christ.

The Face of an Angel

Luke originally introduced Stephen in the list of the seven men chosen to take care of the complaint concerning the daily serving of food. Stephen was described as a man "full of faith and of the Holy Spirit" and "grace and power" (Acts 6:5, 8). The one word aptly expressing the life of Stephen was the word "full." Because he was open to divine influences (so the word "full" implies), Stephen rises above the level of Christian mediocrity and is held up as a wonderful Christian role model.

In Jerusalem, Stephen took his place as a soldier of Christ. He proclaimed the saving message of the gospel and performed miracles by the power of God. But while he preached, certain Jewish men holding Roman citizenship ("Freedmen") challenged his teachings. Their arguments were no match for Stephen's wisdom. After Stephen exposed their ignorance, they resorted to less than honorable tactics to fight Stephen's teachings. They induced men to misrepresent Stephen and thereby stirred up the crowd. Consequently, the Jewish leaders brought Stephen before the Council.

Stephen's accusers put forward false witnesses, and their charges against him were based upon half-truths. Stephen was guilty of stating that Jesus would one day destroy the temple and would alter the customs of the Law of Moses. Paul would later write that the old law was nailed to the cross (Colossians 2:14). Thus the New Testament succeeded the Old Testament (Hebrews 8-9). Salvation was no longer based upon Mosaic law, but was through faith in Christ Jesus (Galatians 3:2). However, Stephen was not guilty of blasphemy. He preached Christ as the end of the law and the beginning of liberty. The charges made against Stephen were of the same nature as those made against Jesus (Matthew 26:57-67). Stephen's accusers unknowingly paid him a beautiful compliment, because their charges against Stephen confirmed his allegiance to Jesus.

The attitudes of Stephen and of those before whom he stood were striking in their contrasts. One extreme was the attitude of the mob. Being "stirred up," they "dragged" Stephen away (Acts 6:12), and the Council fixed their eyes on him.

The other extreme was the attitude of Stephen. He had an apparent inner calmness externalized as the "face of an angel" (Acts 6:15). It was as obvious as the face of Moses that shone when he came down from Mount Sinai after receiving the Ten Commandments (Exodus 34:29-35). Throughout his ordeal, there is not the slightest indication Stephen put up a fight or threatened the mob as they dragged him away. He had no bitterness in his heart, but stood as an innocent lamb before a pack of wolves. Stephen's composure was like Jesus' composure. Peter wrote in 1 Peter 2:21-23:

> For you have been called for this purpose, since Christ also suffered for you, leaving you an example for you to follow in His steps, Who committed no sin, nor was any deceit found in His mouth; and while being reviled, He did not revile in return; while suffering, He uttered no threats, but kept entrusting Himself to Him who judges righteously.

Whatever the "face of an angel" meant, it was certain Stephen was under the influence of a different power (Philippians 4:4-7).

Lessons in Church History

Stephen was permitted by the Council to defend himself against the charges brought against him. Acts 7 records what he said. Stephen's defense revealed additional clues motivating his faithful witness for Christ. Five main themes surfaced in Stephen's defense that undoubtedly fueled his motivation and will also lead every Christian toward new insights in his service to God:

(1) The history recorded in the Old Testament is true. Throughout his defense, Stephen rehearsed many of the great events of Israel's past. He began with the history of Israel's formation: the call of Abraham

out of Ur of the Chaldees (Genesis 12). What follows next were nothing more than those great events of Bible history that have captivated people for centuries:

- The promise God made to the three great patriarchs: Abraham, Isaac and Jacob.

- How God providentially worked in the life of Joseph to save His people from a famine.

- The time a new king arose in the land of Egypt and made the Israelites slaves.

- When Moses led the great company of God's people out of bondage and into the Promised Land.

- The time the Israelites made the golden calf at the foot of Mount Sinai.

- How Joshua led the conquest of the land of Canaan.

- How David, being favored by God, longed to build God a temple.

- When Solomon constructed a beautiful temple and dedicated it to God.

Upon careful reflection, we get the strong impression these notable events were not just some childhood stories. Stephen knew these people really lived and these events actually happened. These were no fairy tales reserved strictly for children's bedtime stories. They were and continue to be a part of the historical heritage of every Christian!

(2) God works in history. Stephen began his defense with a theological truth, "The God of glory appeared" (Acts 7:2). Stephen saw history as theology. He realized God was at work in the world, accomplishing His will. This belief was reinforced when Stephen saw the "glory of God" (v. 55) before he died. God was the One who called for Abraham to leave his country, gave circumcision as the sign of His covenant, and caused Joseph to prosper in the land of Egypt. God was

also responsible for Israel's liberation from Egyptian oppression. Stephen knew this same God was his God, and Stephen freely submitted to whatever way God chose to use him. After Gabriel appeared to Mary and told her she was going to give birth to the Savior of the world, Mary humbly said, "Behold, the bondslave of the Lord; be it done to me according to your word" (Luke 1:38). Stephen possessed this same attitude of submission.

(3) God is not confined to any one place. The Jews were so attached to their country and to their temple they began to behave as though God were confined to the borders of Palestine. This belief was not the teaching of the Old Testament scripture. Solomon admitted in his dedication prayer of the temple, "But will God indeed dwell on the earth? Behold, heaven and the highest heaven cannot contain Thee, how much less this house which I have built!" (1 Kings 8:27). God cannot be caged. Jewish history showed this to be true. God was in Ur of the Chaldees, Egypt, Babylon and in Palestine. Stephen's God was the supreme God over heaven and the earth (Acts 7:48-50).

(4) God has unprecedented patience. God gives His people every advantage. He gave His law to guide them, His love to inspire them, and His prophets to exhort them. Despite all God had done, His people still treated Him with contempt. Peter was right when he said, "The Lord is not slow about His promise, as some count slowness, but is patient toward you, not wishing for any to perish but for all to come to repentance" (2 Peter 3:9). Stephen knew first-hand God's love because God had been patient toward him.

(5) Humankind often rejects what would bless them. This trend can be charted throughout the history of Israel. Stephen knew this to be true. He showed the Council how their forefathers had rejected Moses, God's deliverer. Even after Moses led the Israelites out of bondage, the people continued to dishonor God by challenging Moses' leadership (Numbers 12). Their forefathers also rejected God's servants, the prophets, whom God sent with "living oracles" (Acts 7:38) time and time again. Stephen had learned the lessons from the past and was convinced that people must listen attentively to the message of God.

Hate the Sin, Love the Sinner

Confrontations are never pleasant, but there are times when sin's true identity must be exposed. Sin separates people from God, and sin brings spiritual death; therefore, preachers, teachers and all Christian men and women must not be afraid to confront it (Isaiah 59:1-2; Romans 6:23). Stephen wasn't afraid.

Stephen had the courage to call unrighteousness sin. The attitude of his Jewish brethren was sinful, and their stubbornness would keep them from enjoying God's favor. Sometimes the truth does hurt. Stephen wasn't being harsh or self-righteous. Drastic measures must be taken when mild ones are proven inadequate.

Some acquaintances of mine were heartbroken over their rebellious teenager. He had gotten mixed up in drugs and alcohol, bringing chaos and misery to his parents. His parents talked with him, loved him, and tried to help in every way they knew how, but to no avail. Finally his parents decided they needed to take some drastic actions to force their teenage boy to face the consequences of his own unfortunate choices. Their son had the habit of coming home at all hours of the night inebriated or high. This particular night, however, was going to be different. His parents locked all the doors and windows. When their son came home in a stupor, he was unable to enter. He was told he could not come home unless his attitude changed. Needless to say, he finally came to his senses. These Jews were committing the same error as their forefathers. If they continued in their rebellion, they would forfeit their own salvation.

Stephen also had the courage to tell the truth. By rejecting the gospel, his countrymen had become by association the betrayers and murderers of Jesus. To reject the vicarious death of Christ was to render it ineffective. Were they prepared to accept the consequences of their actions? Paul, like Stephen, had the courage to rebuke the Galatians for abandoning the gospel. Some may have resented his firm stand. Paul knew this would happen and so he wrote, "Have I therefore become your enemy by telling you the truth?" (Galatians 4:16). We all at one time or another need correction. One of the greatest blessings ever to come our way is for another to love us enough to confront us when we are in error. Stephen's deep concern for his countrymen dared him to be courageous.

A Heavenly Home

Stephen's sermon pierced the hearts of those who heard. This piercing was quite different from the experience recorded in Acts 2:38. There, those who heard Peter's message were convicted with the truth of the gospel. Their response, "Brethren, what shall we do?" (v. 37), showed this to be true. However, those to whom Stephen spoke were enraged. They rushed upon him, dragged him out of the city, and stoned him.

In contrast to these brutal actions, Stephen beholds before him what he has been seeing by faith throughout his Christian walk – the glory of God in heaven. That one glimpse into heaven was a tribute to his faith and indicative of his heavenly orientation. Stephen had made the decision in his life to fasten his mind on heaven. Every child of God should have a heavenly orientation. "If then you have been raised up with Christ, keep seeking the things above, where Christ is, seated at the right hand of God. Set your mind on the things above, not on the things that are on the earth. For you have died and your life is hidden with Christ in God" (Colossians 3:1-3).

Not only did Stephen have a vision of heaven, but he also knew his final destination would be there. There was no doubt in his mind about his salvation. Jesus had promised eternal salvation to those who were willing to obey Him (Hebrews 5:8-9). Stephen trusted in that promise and therefore prayed just before he died, "Lord Jesus, receive my spirit!"

Stephen's life was a reflection of the life of Christ. During the final moments of His life, Jesus uttered two prayers. "Father, forgive them; for they do not know what they are doing," He prayed while being crucified. When death was imminent, Jesus prayed, "Father, into Thy hands I commit My spirit" (Luke 23:34, 46). Stephen uttered the same two prayers. Stephen willingly followed Christ's example. He truly possessed the Spirit of Christ.

The Faith Within

What is in the mind of a martyr? In Stephen's case it was a calm composure in the face of an angry attack, a keen consciousness of God's work in history, an uncanny courage rooted in the truth, and a charged conviction predicated upon the promises of God. Consequently, Stephen freely gave his life for Jesus. His death is a rebuke to any shallow commitment to Jesus. Would we be willing to live or die as Stephen did? But Stephen's life is also an encouragement and an inspiration. If he had the courage to live and die for Jesus, so can we. If we possess the faith, would we not have the courage to die for it?

Power Thoughts for Group Discussion

1. To what was Paul referring when he said Christ's death "canceled out the certificate of debt consisting of decrees against us and which was hostile to us; and He has taken it out of the way, having nailed it to the cross" (Colossians 2:14)?

2. Jesus and Stephen chose not to retaliate when wronged. Why? Were they putting themselves at risk by adopting such a position?

3. How has God shown patience toward you?

4. Why is truth such an unwelcome friend to many people? How do people try to avoid the truth?

5. Jesus said to the church in Smyrna, "Be faithful until death, and I will give you the crown of life" (Revelation 2:10). Does "faithful until death" mean be faithful until you die or be faithful if you're threatened with death? Would you truly be willing to die for Jesus?

Chapter 9

The Courage to Live

Acts 9:1-9

"Lives of great men all remind us
We can make our lives sublime.
And, departing, leave behind us
Footprints on the sands of time."
Longfellow

At the age of 4 my oldest daughter was a skeptic. She took issue with everything anyone said. If I told her not to jump on her bed because she might fall and hurt herself, she would reply, "No, I won't." If I told her that eating too much candy might make her sick, she would counter, "No, it won't." If I warned her that what she was about to touch was hot, she would protest, "No, it's not." I was right, of course. She did fall off the bed and hurt herself. Her tummy began to feel sick after she ate too much candy. Her mother kissed her burned finger after I warned her. Just think of all the grief she could have avoided if only she had listened to her dad. My wife and I, on many occasions, have jokingly agreed that given the chance, she would argue with a brick wall.

I believe children are naturally skeptical. They must learn many truths on their own. However, my daughter is not a skeptic any longer. Her experiences have convinced her that beds, candy and hot things can sometimes harm her. Now she's singing my song to her younger brother. But he won't listen, either. Like his sister, he must also discover truth for himself.

Hope for Skeptics

Frank Morison, in his book *Who Moved the Stone*, comments in the preface, "In one sense it [his book] could have taken no other [form], for it is essentially a confession, the inner story of a man who originally set out to write one kind of book and found himself compelled by the sheer force of circumstances to write another." Originally, Morison set out to write the truth about the historical Jesus. He wanted to peel away what he believed was the Jesus of legends and folklore to get to the historical Jesus. Morison believed the miracle stories – particularly the resurrection – were only fiction. However, an amazing thing happened. Morison emerged from his investigation with a conclusion he sought to disprove.

Now convinced of the truthfulness of Jesus' resurrection, Morison titled his first chapter, "A Book That Refused to Be Written." His book delineates those reasons moving him from skepticism to belief.

Saul, who later became the apostle Paul, went through a similar process. Although he initially persecuted the church of Jesus Christ, Saul later emerged as one of the church's most ardent defenders. What produced such a radical change in Saul's life? To help answer this question, we will need to pay close attention to Saul's steps toward faith in Jesus as detailed in Acts 9:1-31.

Fighting Jesus

Luke introduced Saul as one who approved the stoning of Stephen. The mob that picked up stones to throw at Stephen laid their garments at Saul's feet (Acts 7:58). Was Saul their ringleader? He could have been. He was certainly an aspiring young leader determined to keep Judaism free from the influence of heretics like Stephen.

Saul's rampage threatened the existence of the church in Jerusalem. Luke wrote: "And Saul was in hearty agreement with putting him [Stephen] to death. And on that day a great persecution arose against the church in Jerusalem; and they were all scattered throughout the regions of Judea and Samaria, except the apostles" (Acts 8:1).

Saul's determination led him beyond Jerusalem to distant cities like Damascus. Luke continues to describe Saul's rampage in Acts 9:1-2:

"Now Saul, still breathing threats and murder against the disciples of the Lord, went to the high priest, and asked for letters from him to the synagogues at Damascus, so that if he found any belonging to the Way, both men and women, he might bring them bound to Jerusalem."

Saul is pictured as a determined religious zealot, doing what he wanted and doing what he thought was best. Soon, however, Saul's rampage would come to a sudden halt.

Terror gripped the Christians in Damascus when they heard Saul was coming. What would they do? Where would they go to escape? Who could defeat this madman?

Facing the Facts

At midday, as Saul was marching to Damascus, the glory of Jesus knocked him to his knees. A brilliant blaze of light blinded him. A voice penetrated the inner depths of his soul: "Saul, Saul, why are you persecuting Me?" Saul responded in fear, "Who art Thou, Lord?"

The answer was horrifying: "I am Jesus whom you are persecuting." Imagine the shock and fear. Jesus was not dead as Saul had believed. Christians were not religious heretics as he once thought. It's true! Jesus is alive; He is the Son of God. "[T]he angry bull," wrote Warren Wiersbe, "had now become a docile lamb" (112).

The text says Saul, after arriving in Damascus, didn't eat or drink for three days, but prayed constantly. Saul's insides were now being ripped apart by the truth he had just experienced.

Saul learned many truths that day on the road to Damascus. First, he understood the story of the resurrection of Jesus was not religious heresy; it was true. He himself had spoken to Jesus. He now understood Jesus was the Messiah even he was longing to see but had failed to recognize. Saul was also hit with the realization he had been persecuting the very people of God.

Another truth that must have shocked him was the fact that Stephen (whom he formerly witnessed being stoned to death) was right. That meant Saul had been wrong; he had been a servant of Satan, not God. It was time now for Saul to be honest with the truth. Saul's shocking experience led him to the next step in his move from skepticism to belief.

Finding Jesus

How did Saul find Jesus? He found Jesus through the gospel. While Saul was fasting and praying, Jesus appeared to a Christian man in Damascus named Ananias. After assuring Ananias of Saul's change of heart, Jesus sent him to Saul to tell him what he had to do. The way Saul found Jesus is the same way all people find Him – all must come face to face with the truthfulness of Jesus' death, burial and resurrection. These truths are the heart of the gospel (2 Thessalonians 2:13-14). Response to the gospel included such demands as faith (Romans 10:17), repentance (2 Corinthians 7:9-10), a confession of faith in Christ (Romans 10:9-10), and an immersion in water – baptism (Acts 22:16; Romans 6:3-4). Saul didn't waste any time getting himself right with God. He swallowed a lot of self-righteousness. Those who face Jesus will do no less!

Second, Saul would discover the meaning of Christian discipleship. God had a unique mission especially designed for him. Concerning Saul, Jesus said to Ananias in Acts 9:15: "Go, for he is a chosen instrument of Mine, to bear My name before the Gentiles and kings and the sons of Israel." Acts chapters 13-28 record many of Saul's missionary tours throughout the Roman world.

Finally, Saul would discover the meaning of true discipleship. Although at one time Saul was a rising star in the Jewish religion, he would eventually learn true discipleship involved suffering and adversity. Jesus said, "I will show him how much he must suffer for My name's sake" (Acts 9:16). Later, Saul (Paul) wrote true Christian ministry derives its strength from God, not from anything received from other people (2 Corinthians 12:9). In fact, suffering for the cause of Jesus is a mark of authenticity. Notice how Saul differentiates himself from the pseudo-apostles of his day. He wrote:

> Are they servants of Christ? ... I more so; in far more labors, in far more imprisonments, beaten times without number, often in danger of death. Five times I received from the Jews thirty-nine lashes. Three times I was beaten with rods, once I was stoned, three times I was shipwrecked, a night and a day I have spent in the deep. I have been on frequent journeys, in dangers from rivers, dangers from robbers, dangers

from my countrymen, dangers from the Gentiles, dangers
in the city, dangers in the wilderness, dangers on the sea,
dangers among false brethren; I have been in labor and hard-
ship, through many sleepless nights, in hunger and thirst,
often without food, in cold and exposure. Apart from such
external things, there is the daily pressure upon me of concern for all the churches (2 Corinthians 11:23-28).

Isn't the change that takes place in Saul's life ironic? The man who
had everything going for him now rejoices when everything seems to
be going against him. Paul's encounter with the truth moved him toward the third and final step in his life of faith.

Preaching Jesus

Immediately after his conversion, Saul began preaching about Jesus.
Now convinced of Jesus' divinity, he took every opportunity to tell people that Jesus is the Son of God. But many who heard Saul were confounded. Luke records the shock: "And all those hearing him continued to be amazed, and were saying, 'Is this not he who in Jerusalem
destroyed those who call on this name, and who had come here for the
purpose of bringing them bound before the chief priests?'" (Acts 9:21).

The more Saul's motives and actions were called into question, the
more his strength and determination increased. The man who once attempted to prove the falsehood of Christianity now possessed the faith
of Christianity. Something had to be done.

If Saul continued preaching, the Jewish movement to eliminate this
heretical group of Christians would fail. In haste the church's opponents
crafted a plan to get rid of him, now convinced Saul had committed trea-
son. He must be stopped! Secretly, a plan was agreed upon. Certain Jews
would wait at the gates of Damascus for Saul to leave, and when they
saw him they would kill him. However, the plot leaked out. The Christians
in Damascus quickly took Saul and, late one night, lowered him down
the side of the city wall in a basket. Saul then escaped to Jerusalem. The
man who once pursued Christians, was now pursued by the Jews. His
supporters had become his adversaries. What an abrupt change this was!

After arriving in Jerusalem, Saul didn't receive much of a reception.
Although he was a Christian now, many of the disciples were still afraid

of him and would not associate with him. Some thought perhaps Saul was attempting to overtake them by stealth. But a Christian man named Barnabas took Saul, introduced him to the apostles, and told them everything that had happened to Saul. While in Jerusalem, Saul continued to preach and teach. Many of the Jews in Jerusalem plotted to kill him, and again Saul was forced to escape for his life.

Saul was not a skeptic any longer. He was now a true believer. His convictions brought upon him much adversity. Saul tasted for the first time what it was like to be persecuted. Such persecution is often the mark of true Christian discipleship. "To suffer persecution is to be paid the greatest of compliments," wrote William Barclay, "because it is the certain proof that men think we really matter" (75).

Saul, like Morison, began a quest to expose the fallacy of the Christian movement. Each, however, became convinced of the truth they originally tried to disprove. Each did an about-face. Morison never intended to write a book on the truthfulness of Jesus' resurrection. Likewise, Saul never could have imagined he would be a part of the Christian movement. It was a life he refused to live, but he lived such a life – and what a life it was!

Power Thoughts for Group Discussion

1. What forces were at work in your move toward faith in Jesus?

2. Was there ever a time when you thought you were right, although you learned later you were really wrong? How did you feel when you finally realized you were wrong? What did you do?

3. Was Paul considered saved (i.e., cleansed of sins) before or after his baptism? Read Acts 22:16; Acts 2:38; and 1 Peter 3:21. Discuss the significance of baptism.

4. Why did the Christians in Jerusalem doubt the genuineness of Paul's conversion? Do such doubts about others ever surface in the church today? What lessons can you learn from the actions of Barnabas in Acts 9:26-27?

5. Why did Saul begin preaching the gospel immediately after his conversion? Should such behavior be typical of all Christians?

Chapter 10

The Courage to Learn

"The ideal condition would be, I admit, that men should be right by instinct; but since we are all likely to go astray, the reasonable thing is to learn from those who can teach."
Sophocles

M y parents divorced when I was 5 years old. I was much too young to understand what had happened between my mother and father, yet I knew my small world was changing rapidly. I lived with my mother and spent most of the summers with my father. Unfortunately, it wasn't long until I became a notorious brat. I was the bully in school, the class clown, and the child every mother prayed she wouldn't have. The repeated telephone calls my mother received from the principal of my school wearied her. "Your son is out of control," the principal would say. "I must expel him from school." If I was behaving this way during my elementary school days, what would I be like when I became a teenager? Now, my mother and I shudder when we think of such a horrible thought.

When I look back upon those days when I terrorized everyone, I see a desperate little boy crying out for help. It wasn't as if I was lacking in any material or emotional needs. I had parents, although divorced, who I knew loved me and gave me practically anything I wanted. But what I wanted, and what I was given, wasn't really what I needed.

The moment that forever changed my life came after I got angry with my mother one day and went berserk. I can't recall exactly the nature of our argument, but I do remember my mother snatching my arm and hauling me off to my bedroom where I received an unforgettable thrashing. After it was over, while my mother clutched the injured hand she had used as a rod of correction, I looked at her, and to her surprise I said, "Thanks, Mama, I needed that." I was pleading for someone to bring me under control and set me straight when I behaved the way I did. I needed discipline – I finally got it, and now my whole life is better because of it.

Confusing Wants and Needs

What we want is not always what we need. We may want more money, when we really need a budget. We may want to spend, when we really need to save. We may want more time to ourselves, when we really need to give more time to others. We may want more privileges, when we really need to be more responsible. It's easy to confuse perceived needs with genuine needs.

Jesus amassed a large following after He miraculously fed more than 5,000 people with just five barley loaves and two fish. The crowd, however, was more interested in Jesus providing their next meal than they were in His religious teachings. Jesus chided their lack of perception when He said: "Truly, truly, I say to you, you seek Me, not because you saw signs, but because you ate of the loaves, and were filled. Do not work for the food which perishes, but for the food which endures to eternal life, which the Son of Man shall give to you, for on Him the Father, even God, has set His seal" (John 6:26-27).

Physical food, although important, was not what the crowd really needed. They needed to feast upon the words of the One who said, "I am the bread of life; he who comes to Me shall not hunger, and he who believes in Me shall never thirst" (John 6:35).

Jesus gives to us just what we need. In Acts 8:1-40, we find three accounts of how Jesus satisfies the real needs of people. Some of these needs are obvious and some are not so obvious. We will be surprised to learn what these needs were, which are also the common needs of all people, and just how they were and continue to be satisfied in Jesus Christ.

A Family Feud

Before Saul became a Christian, he initiated a "great persecution" against the church and many of the Christians in Jerusalem were scattered throughout the surrounding countryside (Acts 8:1-2). Fellow Christians buried their beloved brother Stephen who was the first person to be killed for being a Christian. The hostility escalated to the point that Saul "began ravaging the church, entering house after house; and dragging off men and women, he would put them in prison" (v. 3). The irony was the more the church was persecuted the more the church grew in numbers and strength. Like wind blowing seed, this persecution scattered the seeds of the gospel into such regions as Judea and Samaria, as those who fled from Jerusalem went everywhere "preaching the word" (v. 4).

Keep in mind Jesus had said earlier to His disciples that they were to be His witnesses "both in Jerusalem, and in all Judea and Samaria, and even to the remotest part of the earth" (Acts 1:8). A new expansion of Jesus' commission began here. Philip, one of the deacons of the Jerusalem church, came to the city of Samaria, and began preaching about Jesus. This move was significant on Philip's part. What's so significant about Philip preaching in the city of Samaria? To better understand, we need to know something about Samaria's history.

The proverb, "Jews have no dealings with Samaritans," was common during Jesus' day (John 4:9). Not only did Jews and Samaritans avoid each other, but they also despised each other. The city of Samaria was located in the region called Samaria. This region sat squarely in the middle of Palestine, separating the regions of Galilee to the north and Judea to the south, on the west side of the Jordan River. If a Jew desired to go from Galilee to Judea or from Judea to Galilee, he would not pass through Samaria, the quickest and easiest route. Instead, he would cross the Jordan River, travel through Perea on the eastern side of the Jordan River, a much longer and more difficult journey, and cross the river again, arriving at his destination. To say that the Jews had no dealings with the Samaritans was an understatement.

Why was there such enmity between them? The story begins back in 1 Kings 12 when the nation of Israel split into two separate and warring factions. Rehoboam, after the death of his father, Solomon, planned to rule the entire nation with an iron fist. He said: "My father made your yoke heavy, but I will add to your yoke; my father disciplined you with whips, but I will discipline you with scorpions" (1 Kings 12:14).

Needless to say, such harsh words set off a chain reaction. In frustration, 10 tribes, led by Jeroboam, seceded from the nation of Israel. Jeroboam formed what came to be known as the northern kingdom or the kingdom of Israel. Samaria became the capital city. Rehoboam maintained control over the kingdom of Judah with Jerusalem as the capital city. These two kingdoms were constantly at each other's throats, neither trusting the other.

The Assyrians conquered the kingdom of Israel in 722 B.C., overthrew Samaria, and deported much of the population to Assyria. The region was repopulated with other, non-Jewish nationalities. Eventually, the Jews left in the region intermarried with these foreigners and became what we may call a mixed breed of people – Samaritans (2 Kings 16:10-17:41).

Nearly 140 years later, Nebuchadnezzar, king of Babylon, overran the kingdom of Judah. The Babylonians levelled Jerusalem and carried the Jews into exile. After 70 years of captivity, the Persians (the new power on the world scene) allowed the Jews to return to their homeland and gave them permission to rebuild the city of Jerusalem and the temple. The excitement could not be contained! Even the Samaritans heard about their good fortune. As the Jews returned to begin reconstruction, many of the Samaritans asked the Jews if they could participate in this thrilling endeavor. Perhaps this could have been a grand opportunity to lay aside the hostility once and for all and begin a new and united partnership. The Samaritans requested: "Let us build with you, for we, like you, seek your God; and we have been sacrificing to Him since the days of Esarhaddon king of Assyria, who brought us up here" (Ezra 4:2).

The Jews responded harshly to their request: "You have nothing in common with us in building a house to our God; but we ourselves will together build to the Lord God of Israel" (Ezra 4:3).

Outraged by the arrogance of the Jews, the Samaritans launched a campaign to dissuade the Jews from rebuilding their city. The Samaritans tried everything within their power to discourage and frighten the Jews, and the wedge between the two groups naturally widened.

After a while, the Samaritans finally withdrew and formed their own community. They had their own religion, their own law, and erected their own temple on Mount Gerizim. According to Josephus, a Jewish historian, the Samaritans were once again the victim of prejudicial assault. In 128 B.C., a Jew named John Hyrcanus scaled Mount Gerizim and reduced the Samaritan temple to rubble and the city of Samaria to a memory. Josephus writes:

> And when Hyrcanus had taken the city, which was not done till after a year's siege, he was not contented with doing that only, but he demolished it entirely, and brought rivulets to it to drown it, for he dug such hollows as might let the waters run under it; nay, he took away the very marks that there had ever been such a city there (*Antiquities of the Jews*, XIII, X, 3).

It's Not Easy Being an Outcast

Don't you feel sorry for the Samaritans? If people have ever rejected you because of your nationality, color, speech, profession, gender or your size, then you know exactly what it must have been like to be a Samaritan. Rejection for the Samaritans was a way of life. That's why the Samaritan woman was so surprised when Jesus asked her for a drink of water. She replied, "How is it that You, being a Jew, ask me for a drink since I am a Samaritan woman?" (John 4:9). It wasn't long before the Samaritan woman had the whole city of Sychar coming to find out who this Jesus really was. Jesus came telling the Samaritans they too were important to God.

Philip, like Jesus, brought the message of the Lord to a disillusioned people. The dreams, the aspirations and the hopes of the Samaritans had long been shattered. Their frantic search for purpose and self-worth had made them vulnerable to one of the greatest tricksters of the day – Simon (whom we'll discuss in the next section). Philip marched into the city of Samaria and preached the gospel to them.

> And the multitudes with one accord were giving attention to what was said by Philip, as they heard and saw the signs which he was performing. For in the case of many who had

unclean spirits, they were coming out of them shouting with
a loud voice; and many who had been paralyzed and lame
were healed (Acts 8:6-7).

"At last, somebody cares!" was the cry of joy throughout all Samaria.
It was true; somebody really did care. Jesus believes everyone is important. After such a long history of rejection, this message of ac-
ceptance was just what the Samaritans genuinely needed. No wonder
people across the world continue to sing, "Jesus loves me this I know,
for the Bible tells me so."

Do Not Covet

Simon's case was completely different than the Samaritans. Simon
basked in his escalating popularity. Who wouldn't relish the thought
of being called the "Great Power of God" (Acts 8:10)? He had the
Samaritans eating right out of his hands. Simon was a masterful ma-
gician and his magical tricks astonished everyone. When he heard
the message of Philip, Simon believed, along with many of the
Samaritans, and was baptized. What seemed to catch Simon's real interest, however, were the spectacular miracles being wrought by Philip.
Simon was amazed and carefully watched for the hidden source of power behind Philip's ability to perform miracles. It was all he could think
about. Simon wanted to perform real miracles like Philip, not just as-
tound people with magical tricks.

Once the news about Philip's progress reached the apostles in Jerusalem,
Peter and John were immediately dispatched to Samaria to help stabi-
lize the work. When they arrived, Peter and John prayed for the Samaritans
and began laying their hands upon them so they could receive the miraculous power of the Holy Spirit. Such power would assist the Samaritans
in building up the church in their area and would also serve as a constant
confirmation of the message they would proclaim.

As Simon observed Peter and John, he discovered how Philip obtained
the power to work miracles: "Now when Simon saw that the Spirit was
bestowed through the laying on of the apostles' hands, he offered them
money, saying, 'Give this authority to me as well, so that everyone on
whom I lay my hands may receive the Holy Spirit' " (Acts 8:18).

Peter sternly rebuked Simon:

> May your silver perish with you, because you thought you
> could obtain the gift of God with money! You have no part
> or portion in this matter, for your heart is not right before
> God. Therefore repent of this wickedness of yours, and pray
> the Lord that if possible, the intention of your heart may be
> forgiven you. For I see that you are in the gall of bitter-
> ness and in the bondage of iniquity (Acts 8:20-23).

Simon coveted the power of the Holy Spirit and wanted to use the power to his own advantage, but what he needed was for someone to reprimand him because of his lack of integrity.

Give people enough time and eventually their true character will sur-face. Simon wasn't as interested in helping people as he was in manip-ulating them. He wasn't interested so much in being religious as he was interested in using religion to suit his own purposes. Simon's behavior was like many of the Pharisees who were more interested in being es-teemed by their peers than they were in being right with God (John 12:43).

People like Simon should be rebuked and shown for what they real-ly are – those who hold "to a form of godliness, although they have de-nied its power" (2 Timothy 3:5). Again, in the case of Simon, the mes-sage of Jesus touched a genuine need. Often, when people encounter for the first time the depth of wickedness lodged within their own hearts, it's enough to make them want to change. Hopefully, Simon did change when he asked Peter to pray for him.

We may be surprised by the number of "Simons" in the church. They aren't bad people; they're just misdirected. Their priorities are all mixed up. The real significance of what Christianity is all about has somehow eluded them. We may hear of a church Simon using his or her free-will contribution as a leverage to ensure support for personal agendas. We may see a church Simon behaving like a Christian at worship assem-blies on Sundays, but mimicking the behavior of a pagan during the week. Church Simons are not difficult to spot. Jesus could spot them a mile away. "Hypocrites," He called them (Matthew 23). What can we do about the little Simon in us? The best way to ward off the spirit of Simon is to perpetually keep our motives pure.

Keep It Simple

Philip's preaching tour in Samaria was a tremendous success. He had bridged the gap between Jew and Samaritan. As he and the apostles returned to Jerusalem, the angel of the Lord spoke to Philip, saying: "Arise and go south to a road that descends from Jerusalem to Gaza" (Acts 8:26). Philip quickly obeyed the Lord's direction, and to his amazement, he came across an Ethiopian eunuch reading scripture while sitting in his chariot. It's evident the Ethiopian was a very religious man. He had traveled more than 200 miles to worship in Jerusalem. "Do you understand what you are reading?" Philip inquired. "Well, how could I, unless someone guides me?" the Ethiopian responded. The Ethiopian then invited Philip to study with him (vv. 27-31).

"I'm confused," was the real admission of the Ethiopian. I enjoy having people in my home for Bible study. One year I called my weekly Bible studies "Tuesday Night Live." I had one purpose – to get people to read the Bible on a daily basis.

There were no assigned readings. Each person was free to read as much or as little of the Bible as desired. What was required, however, was that each one share with the group what was read, why it was read, and how the reading affected him or her. Without fail, most of the studies centered on passages in the Bible that were confusing to someone. Many would comment about their readings, "I'm confused, and I don't know if I really understand what's being talked about." It was thrilling to see, after such questions were discussed and studied, each person come to understand the meaning of the passage. You could sense a feeling of pure joy: "So that's what it means, it all makes sense now. How could I have ever missed it?"

The Ethiopian was reading a passage from the prophet Isaiah:

> He was led as a sheep to slaughter;
> And as a lamb before its shearer is silent,
> So He does not open His mouth.
> In humiliation His judgment was taken away;
> Who shall relate His generation?
> For His life is removed from the earth (Acts 8:32-33).

The Ethiopian's question, "[O]f whom does the prophet say this? Of himself, or of someone else?", bares his bewilderment. Philip began at that reading and taught the Ethiopian how the passage related to Jesus Christ. "That's it!" the Ethiopian may have exclaimed while he and Philip rode along in the chariot. "I understand now; it all makes perfect sense. Stop the chariot! Look, Philip, here's water, I want to be baptized!" (Acts 8:36, paraphrased). After the Ethiopian confessed Jesus was the Son of God, Philip baptized him, and the Ethiopian went on his way rejoicing! How fascinating it is to observe how the Ethiopian not only understood the passage, but was also led to Jesus and discovered the plan of Jesus demanded he be baptized for the remission of sins (2:38). All the Ethiopian needed was for someone to help him sort through his confusion.

When I was in the insurance and investment business, my supervisors schooled me in the "K.I.S.S." ("Keep It Simple Stupid") principle. My game plan was to educate, not confuse, the potential client. I've carried this same philosophy over into my ministry. People are already confused about religion. They don't need someone else to come along with new theories, pseudo revelations or opinions. What people need is a presentation of the pure Word of Christ, stripped of any human embellishments. Once again the message of Jesus fulfilled a genuine need. "Tell me the story of Jesus," says the gospel song, "write on my heart every word."

The Heart of the Matter

In the accounts of the Samaritan woman, Simon and the Ethiopian eunuch, the message of Jesus cut through superficial needs and got right to the heart of the matter. Those who are in a state of despair need to learn how important they are to God. Others, who hide their true motives behind a religious veneer, need to be rebuked and exhorted and learn how to serve God from a genuine heart. And still others, who are in a state of disorientation, need to learn the true and uncomplicated Word of God. Jesus was just what the Samaritans, Simon and the Ethiopian needed. Jesus is just what you need also! Mosie Lister's song, "He Knows Just What I Need," expresses the concern Jesus has for you:

My Jesus knows when I am lonely,
He knows each pain, He sees each tear;
He understands each lonely heartache,
He understands because He cares.

My Jesus knows when I am burdened,
He knows how much my heart can bear;
He lifts me up when I am sinking,
And brings me joy beyond compare.

When other friends seem to forget me,
When skies are dark, when hope is gone;
By faith I feel His arms about me,
And hear Him say, "You're not alone."

My Jesus knows just what I need,
Oh, yes, He knows just what I need;
He satisfies, And ev'ry need supplies,
Yes, He knows just what I need.

Power Thoughts for Group Discussion

1. Why is it so easy to confuse perceived needs with real needs? How do you help people see past their felt needs?

2. If you were Rehoboam, what steps would you have taken to maintain the unity of the kingdom? How could these steps help maintain unity in the church?

3. What verses in the Bible would you share with someone who held a very low view of himself?

4. What other fundamental needs are met in Jesus Christ?

5. Read 2 Peter 3:14-18. How do religious and non-religious people distort the Scriptures today?

Chapter 11

The Courage to Stand

Acts 9:32-11:18

"Stand up, stand up for Jesus!"
George Duffield *(Hymn)*

Remember the massacre in Tiananmen Square? Quite frankly, I don't know how anyone could forget it. Although this tragedy happened over a decade ago, the political repercussions continue to this day. I have kept the story about it in my files. As in the case of any tragedy, there's always something that's memorable. In this case, the news focused upon a Chinese student who captured the attention of the world. A section of an article in the June 19, 1989, issue of *Time* reads:

> One man against an army. The power of the people versus the power of the gun. There he stood, implausibly resolute in his thin white shirt, an unknown Chinese man facing down a lumbering column of tanks. For a moment that will be long remembered, the lone man defined the struggle of China's citizens. "Why are you here?" he shouted at the silent steel hulk. "You have done nothing but create misery. My city is in chaos because of you."
>
> The brief encounter between the man and the tank captured an epochal event in the lives of 1.1 billion Chinese: the state

clanking with menace, swiveling right and left with uncertainty, is halted in its tracks because the people got in its way, and because it got in theirs (9).

The massacre in Tiananmen Square was a ruthless, bloody and appalling display of human brutality. But for a moment, a slight moment, before the exploding of ammunition, a young Chinese man stood as a human blockade. The photograph of the scene in *Time* magazine is impressive. One solitary person brought to a halt four massive tanks containing unbelievable firepower. There he stood, just one person.

The power of just one person is difficult to fathom. One person can set a movement on fire with a dream. One person can lead a failing company to the pinnacle of success. One person can bring renewed optimism to a desolate people. We should never underestimate the power that only one human being can exert. "The work of the individual," said Igor Sikorsky, "still remains the spark that moves mankind forward."

The underlying thesis of Acts 9:32-11:18 is the profound impact an individual can have upon the lives of other people. Such an impact is illustrated by the lives of Peter, Dorcas and Cornelius. Take a look at these three individuals and see for yourself the power of one practically demonstrated.

The Lord Is Merciful

The narrative beginning in Acts 9:32 resumes the story of Peter's activities in Acts 8:24. Earlier, the Jerusalem church had sent Peter and John to Samaria to impart the Holy Spirit upon those who had been baptized. In Samaria, Peter sharply rebuked Simon for camouflaging his wickedness under a cloak of spiritual sincerity. As Peter traveled through the region, he came to Lydda and met a man named Aeneas. Because of his paralysis, Aeneas had been bedridden for eight years. How difficult it must have been to be incapacitated for that length of time! Even today many people endure such extreme immobility. Aeneas' predicament, however, was about to change. "And Peter said to him, 'Aeneas, Jesus Christ heals you; arise, and make your bed' " (Acts 9:34).

"And immediately," Luke records, "he arose." Aeneas' paralysis wasn't psychological; it was a genuine physical problem. His healing, therefore, cannot be compared to the supposed miracles of modern-day faith healers. Aeneas, no doubt, was forever indebted for Peter's interest in him and intervention on his behalf. Peter certainly made a difference in Aeneas' life. As a result of this amazing miracle, many others, convinced now of the validity of the message of Christ, turned to the Lord. Peter's compassion toward Aeneas exemplifies God's compassion toward us. The psalmist said:

The Lord is gracious and merciful;
Slow to anger and great in lovingkindness.
The Lord is good to all,
And His mercies are over all His works. ...
The Lord sustains all who fall,
And raises up all who are bowed down.
The eyes of all look to Thee,
And Thou dost give them their food in due time.
Thou dost open Thy hand,
And dost satisfy the desire of every living thing. ...
The Lord is near to all who call upon Him,
To all who call upon Him in truth
(Psalm 145:8-9, 14-16, 18).

God's compassion didn't end with the healing of Aeneas. In fact, where ever Christians are the compassion of Jesus continues to be felt. A lovely woman named Tabitha (Dorcas in Greek) became extreme-ly ill and died. Her body was cleaned and laid in an upper room of a house. When the Christians in Joppa learned Peter was in Lydda, a near-by city, they immediately sent a couple of men to him. These men begged Peter to return with them to Joppa. In haste, Peter returned with them and entered the upper room where Dorcas was lying. Luke con-tinues the narrative: "But Peter sent them all out and knelt down and prayed, and turning to the body, he said, 'Tabitha, arise.' And she opened her eyes, and when she saw Peter, she sat up" (Acts 9:40).

By the power of Jesus, Tabitha received another opportunity to live. However, this opportunity to live again wasn't relegated solely to the first century. We have a far greater opportunity to live again – an op-portunity that preempts any miraculous physical resurrection. Paul explained it best when he said, "Therefore if any man is in Christ, he is a new creature; the old things passed away; behold, new things have come" (2 Corinthians 5:17). The process of becoming a new creature is simple. Paul described it this way:

> Or do you not know that all of us who have been baptized into Christ Jesus have been baptized into His death? Therefore we have been buried with Him through baptism into death, in order that as Christ was raised from the dead through the glory of the Father, so we too might walk in newness of life (Romans 6:3-4).

"Newness of life" is synonymous with "new creature." Who really needs a physical miracle now when we can receive a new lease on life through a spiritual birth by baptism for the remission of sins? As soon as word of Peter's miracle reached the surrounding community, "many believed [turned to] in the Lord" (Acts 9:42). Any time the practical demonstration of faith is seen, conversions will soon follow.

The Keys of the Kingdom

Peter's activities continued, but now may be a good time to refresh our memory concerning Peter's place in Christ's mission. Jesus told Peter he would receive the "keys of the kingdom" (a figurative expression denoting authority, Matthew 16:19). Thinking back upon the activities of Peter should remind us how he used those keys to open the spiritual gate of God's kingdom for the Jews in Acts 2. He also unlocked the spiritual gate of God's kingdom for the Samaritans in Acts 8. Now in Acts 10, Peter will once again insert the keys into the spiritual lock of God's kingdom and open the gate for Gentiles to enter also. This act by Peter moves the first-century church into the third stage of Jesus' commission: "[Y]ou shall be My witnesses both in Jerusalem, and in all Judea and Samaria, and even to the remotest part of the earth" (Acts 1:8). The remotest part of the earth begins here with the conversion of a man named Cornelius and is later picked up by Paul and his journeys recorded in Acts chapters 13-26.

Cornelius was a Gentile and that fact alone would cause Jews not to associate with him. Gentiles were as repulsive to the Jews as Samaritans.

By divine guidance, Peter responded favorably to the delegation sent to him by Cornelius. When he arrived in Caesarea, Peter entered Cornelius' house. "And opening his mouth, Peter said: 'I most certainly understand now that God is not one to show partiality, but in every nation the man who fears Him and does what is right, is welcome to Him'" (Acts 10:34-35).

Peter then preached the gospel to Cornelius and his household. He and his family, convinced now of the saving grace of Jesus, were baptized. Peter had a profound impact upon Cornelius and the others who were present.

Unfortunately, the brethren in Jerusalem were disappointed in Peter. They weren't as convinced as Peter about the inclusion of Gentiles being God's will. Peter explained to them what had happened and affirmed that his actions were indeed the will of God. Consequently, Peter helped these brethren overcome their ancestral prejudices. Thanks to Peter, they were beginning to understand for the first time the far-reaching effects of God's plan.

Aeneas, Tabitha, Cornelius, the brethren and many others were touched powerfully by one solitary Christian. Peter made a difference in all of their lives, and his influence continues to be felt even today by the example he led and by the epistles he wrote (1, 2 Peter).

Dorcas' Contributions

Dorcas is one of the unsung heroines of the Bible. Little is said about her, but what is said places her in faith's hall of fame. Luke tells the story in a masterful way. The emphasis doesn't seem to be so much upon Peter's actions, but upon the wonderful contributions Dorcas made while she was alive:

> Now in Joppa there was a certain disciple named Tabitha (which translated in Greek is called Dorcas); this woman was abounding with deeds of kindness and charity, which she continually did. And it came about at that time that she fell sick and died; and when they had washed her body, they laid it in an upper room. And since Lydda was near Joppa, the disciples, having heard that Peter was there, sent two men

to him, entreating him, "Do not delay to come to us." And Peter arose and went with them. And when he had come, they brought him into the upper room; and all the widows stood beside him weeping, and showing all the tunics and garments that Dorcas used to make while she was with them. But Peter sent them all out and knelt down and prayed, and turning to the body, he said, "Tabitha, arise." And she opened her eyes, and when she saw Peter, she sat up. And he gave her his hand and raised her up; and calling the saints and widows, he presented her alive (Acts 9:36-41).

Dorcas was truly a model Christian. She continually abounded in deeds of kindness and charity. She stands as the embodiment of Paul's words in 1 Corinthians 15:58: "Therefore, my beloved brethren, be steadfast, immovable, always abounding in the work of the Lord, knowing that your toil is not in vain in the Lord."

The widows showed Peter all the tunics and garments Dorcas had made. This reminds me of a time when I was preaching in east Texas. In the congregation, there was a sweet, elderly lady who crocheted every newborn baby a bonnet for his or her head. She had health problems, her bones were fragile, and she couldn't do very much. She just made bonnets. For years those beautiful bonnets brightened the worship service with rich colors. Every expectant mother couldn't wait to receive one of those beautiful bonnets. The spirit of Dorcas is rare in the extremely impersonal society in which we live. She made a real difference in the lives of many, many people.

When individuals like Dorcas die, they are sorely missed. The widows wept over the death of their dear friend. We need more Christians like Dorcas who are positive forces in the lives of others.

If He Can, We Can Too

Cornelius was a man of integrity. According to Acts 10:2, he is described as being devout, a respecter of God, benevolent and a man of prayer. God heard his prayers, and in a vision informed Cornelius to send for a man named Peter to learn what he must do to be saved. Cornelius quickly dispatched a delegation to Joppa to bring Peter to his house.

In the meantime, Cornelius made preparations for Peter's arrival. He called his relatives and close friends together. And when Peter finally arrived "he entered, and found many people assembled" (Acts 10:27). Cornelius then explained to Peter why he summoned him:

> Four days ago to this hour, I was praying in my house during the ninth hour; and behold, a man stood before me in shining garments, and he said, "Cornelius, your prayer has been heard and your alms have been remembered before God. Send therefore to Joppa and invite Simon, who is also called Peter, to come to you; he is staying at the house of Simon the tanner by the sea." And so I sent to you immediately, and you have been kind enough to come. Now then, we are all here present before God to hear all that you have been commanded by the Lord (Acts 10:30-33).

Without a doubt, Cornelius had a major influence upon his family, his relatives and his friends. He had enough interest in others to make every effort to get people into a position to hear the good news of the gospel. If it were not for the Corneliuses of our lives, we may never have had the opportunity to come to the knowledge of the truth. Remember, even Peter was brought to the Lord by his brother Andrew (John 1:40-41).

Peter, Dorcas and Cornelius dramatically illustrate the powerful effects of individuals. The world will be reached only through individuals, and the church is only as strong as her individual members. Like Peter, we have the greatest message in the entire world to proclaim. The message of the gospel is supported by the resurrection of Jesus, empowered by the Spirit of God, and propelled by God's will and providence. Like Dorcas, our deeds can bring comfort and cheer to others (Matthew 25:31-46). And like Cornelius, our integrity and reputation can exert major influence, motivating people to come to the Lord through our efforts (1 Corinthians 11:1; 1 Peter 3:15).

It's easy to get caught up in the immensity of things: large churches, lots of money, big buildings, global missions, However, if it were not for individuals who take their stand with Jesus, nothing would be accomplished.

The story is told that during World War II, a church in Strasbourg was destroyed. After the bombing, the members of this particular church went to see what was left and found that the entire roof had fallen in, leaving a heap of rubble and broken glass. Much to their surprise, however, a statue of Christ with outstretched hands, having been carved centuries before by a great artist, was still standing erect. It was virtually unharmed except both hands had been sheared off by a falling beam. The people hurried to a sculptor in town and asked if he could replace the hands of the statue. He was willing, and he even offered to do it for nothing. The church officials met to consider the sculptor's proposition and decided not to accept his offer. Why? Because they felt the statue without hands would be the greatest representation possible that God's work is done through His people. How true! We are the spiritual hands of Jesus, and each of us can make a difference.

Power Thoughts for Group Discussion

1. Are the so-called miracles of modern-day faith healers really miraculous in nature? How do their miracles compare to the miracles of Jesus and the apostles?

2. The statement was made in this chapter that "Wherever Christians are, the compassion of Jesus continues to be felt." In what ways could the compassion of Jesus be shown today?

3. The Bible says faith without works is dead (James 2:14-26). What kind of works does James have in mind?

4. Describe the differing methods of reaching (evangelizing) non-Christians in vogue today. Which method, in your opinion, is the most effective? Which method introduced you to the gospel?

5. What factors distinguish the church from other organizations that also help people who are in need?

Chapter 12

The Courage to Unite

Acts 11:19-30

"Then join hand in hand, brave Americans all,
By uniting we stand, by dividing we fall"
John Dickinson *(The Liberty Song, 1768)*

I have a good friend named Leroy. Several years ago he walked into my church office and introduced himself. "Do you have a minute?" he asked. "I just need to talk with someone right now." He explained he was having some problems and inquired if I might have a few moments to pray for and with him. We prayed. Afterwards, Leroy and I visited for at least an hour or two. I found him to be extremely intelligent, witty and compassionate. Since that meeting in my office, Leroy and I have often visited on the telephone. The subjects of our conversations are usually spiritual in nature. We stay abreast of each other's lives; we encourage one another; and we pray for one another.

Leroy is a Christian, and he worships with another congregation. He teaches a Bible class and is extremely interested in developing godly qualities in young people. He loves his family, the church and people in general. When my secretary tells me that Leroy is on the phone, I swell with brotherly love. Although Leroy and I are a lot alike, there is a noticeable difference between us. Leroy is black, and I'm white, but the cross of Jesus has a remarkable way of dissolving our racial and cultural differences. Leroy is my brother in Christ.

Racism is today's catchword. Our nation and the world in general seem to be forever embroiled in conflict. How can people who are so different live together in peace? Is it possible? What's the secret to unity? Acts 11:19-30 captures a wonderful historical event in the life of the early church. Read on – what follows may change your whole life.

A New Name

Long ago, through the prophet Isaiah, God said:

> To them I will give in My house and within My walls a memorial, And a name better than that of sons and daughters; I will give them an everlasting name which will not be cut off. ... For Zion's sake I will not keep silent, And for Jerusalem's sake I will not keep quiet, Until her righteousness goes forth like brightness, And her salvation like a torch that is burning. And the nations will see your righteousness, And all kings your glory; And you will be called by a new name, Which the mouth of the Lord will designate. ... But My servants will be called by another name (Isaiah 56:5; 62:1-2; 65:15).

These passages are intriguing. They are timely words spoken to a distraught people. Although God punished His people for their iniquities, He now promised a new beginning and reassured them saying, "the former troubles are forgotten, And they are hidden from My sight" (Isaiah 65:16). A new name would be the clue indicating the beginning of a new era. This new name would also be an everlasting name. What was Isaiah talking about? What would this new name be? When would this new name be given? These are puzzling questions indeed.

Several new names were suggested in Isaiah's message. For instance, God's people would no longer be called "Forsaken" or "Desolate"; but instead, they would be known as "My delight is in her" and "Married" (Isaiah 62:4). Yet, it's typical of Isaiah's book to contain much more than meets the eye. Perhaps a New Testament passage would shed light on the real identity of this new name. Although it is true that Luke recorded the formation of the church in Antioch, his main objective was to underscore a pivotal event in church history. The text reads:

"[A]nd when he [Barnabas] had found him [Saul], he brought him to Antioch. And it came about that for an entire year they met with the church, and taught considerable numbers; and the disciples were first called Christians in Antioch" (Acts 11:25-26).

Read the closing phrase again: "the disciples were first called Christians in Antioch." Up until this time those who had been following Jesus were known as believers, disciples, saints, brethren and members of the Way. Never before had they been called Christians. "Christian" was a new name. Read again the words of Isaiah. If the church had begun years earlier, why was it at this time in the church's history God's people began to be known as Christians? Some have suggested the term "Christian" was used by pagan neighbors as a contemptuous way of identifying the followers of Christ. Others, however, think the believers in Antioch naturally coined this term to identify themselves. The point of Luke's message is not the identity of the person who may have first spoken the name Christian, but that God through His providence gave the term "Christian." It was a name God chose for His people to wear. Let me now ask a question: Why was the name Christian first applied to the disciples in Antioch and not to the believers in Jerusalem, or in Judea, or even in Samaria?

A New Emphasis

Why were the disciples in Antioch first called Christians? Was it because they were the most dynamic group around? The Antioch church was certainly dynamic. Two of the most beloved men of the Bible, Barnabas and Paul, preached and worked with the church in Antioch. Eventually, Antioch would become the overseeing congregation for Paul and Barnabas when the time came for them to embark on their missionary tours. No doubt about it, Antioch had two of the most effective preachers in the first century. But the Jerusalem church had their noted preachers as well. Peter and John, along with the rest of the apostles, continued working with the church in Jerusalem. Each congregation had respectable and godly leaders.

Could it be the disciples in Antioch were first called Christians because of their explosive growth? Notice the following verses: "And the hand of the Lord was with them, and a large number who believed turned to the Lord. ... And considerable numbers were brought to the Lord. ... [A]nd taught considerable numbers" (Acts 11:21, 24, 26).

When compared to the numerical growth in the Jerusalem church, these numbers lose their punch. Remember that 3,000 were added to the church on the Day of Pentecost when the apostles preached the gospel (Acts 2:41). It wasn't very long until the number of disciples in Jerusalem exceeded 5,000 (4:4). After Acts 4, the number of believers multiplied exceedingly (5:14; 6:1, 7). Within just a few years the followers of Jesus Christ filled Jerusalem.

Maybe Antioch's benevolent and caring attitude was the reason they were the first disciples to be called Christians. According to Acts 11:27-30, Agabus, a first-century prophet, predicted that a famine would hit the land of Palestine and that Judea would be hit especially hard. Motivated by their Christian compassion, the disciples in Antioch contributed money to provide for the needs of their fellow believers living in Judea. However, such benevolence was not unique to Antioch. In fact, the disciples in Jerusalem demonstrated their care for one another when "they began selling their property and possessions, and were sharing them with all, as anyone might have need" (Acts 2:45). They even considered their possessions as common property among them. As needs arose, the believers in Jerusalem "who were owners of land or houses would sell them and bring the proceeds of the sales, and lay them at the apostles' feet; and they would be distributed to each, as any had need" (4:35). The time eventually came when the church in Jerusalem needed a daily distribution of benevolence (6:1). Based upon these facts, Jerusalem was more a model of compassion and concern than Antioch.

Building Bridges

If the issue as to why the disciples in Antioch were first called Christians cannot be explained by referring to those who preached and worked there, the church's growth, or even by the church's marvelous example of compassion, then just what was the reason? The reason is not all that difficult to see. A clue is found in Acts 11:19-20:

> So then those who were scattered because of the persecution that arose in connection with Stephen made their way

to Phoenicia and Cyprus and Antioch, speaking the word to no one except to Jews alone. But there were some of them, men of Cyprus and Cyrene, who came to Antioch and began speaking to the Greeks also, preaching the Lord Jesus.

This passage picks up the story in Acts 8:4 where Luke had temporarily departed from his narrative. If we look closely we will see a contrast between two groups of people, separated by the word "but" in the passage above. Both groups of disciples traveled beyond the land of Palestine preaching the gospel. The difference between the two groups lies in the audiences they addressed. The first group of Jewish disciples preached only to Jews. The second group of Jewish disciples, however, came to Antioch and preached to Greeks (or Gentiles). This action is the first deliberate effort by Jewish believers to preach to Gentiles.

In Acts 10, Cornelius, a Gentile, sent for Peter, a Jew, but Peter had to be conditioned by a vision to understand God's inclusion of the Gentiles. This act by "some of them" demonstrated that Christianity was well on its way to realizing its worldwide mission. The crumbling of the Berlin Wall in 1989 between Western and Eastern Germany doesn't even compare to the collapse of the prejudicial barriers dividing Jews and Gentiles for centuries. But now, in Jesus Christ, Jews and Gentiles were brought together in one church, worshiping side by side as spiritual brothers and sisters. Paul stated the matter plainly: "For you are all sons of God through faith in Christ Jesus. For all of you who were baptized into Christ have clothed yourselves with Christ. There is neither Jew nor Greek, there is neither slave nor free man, there is neither male nor female; for you are all one in Christ Jesus" (Galatians 3:26-28).

Surely the reason the disciples were first called Christians in Antioch was because they had overcome their prejudicial attitudes and had crossed over to meet those who were much different than themselves. "The new way," wrote F. F. Bruce, "was wide enough to accommodate believers of the most diverse backgrounds" (228). Paul would later write: "Therefore from now on we recognize no man according to the flesh" (2 Corinthians 5:16). In the book of Ephesians, Paul referred to the disclosure of a great mystery. What's the great mystery? "To be specific, that the Gentiles are fellow heirs and fellow members of the body, and fellow partakers of the promise in Christ Jesus through the gospel" (Ephesians 3:6). In Jesus Christ, people of the most diverse occupations, intellect, economic standing, nationality and skin color can live together in complete harmony.

New Opportunities

The news about the church in Antioch went forth like flashes of lightening. Before long, Antioch's success reached the Jerusalem church. How would the church in Jerusalem respond? It was only after Peter forcefully argued for the inclusion of the Gentiles when they finally accepted Cornelius and his household as fellow believers (Acts 11:1-18). Would Jerusalem react negatively to Antioch's success? From all appearances, Jerusalem was ecstatic and thrilled about Antioch's progress. To demonstrate their support, the church in Jerusalem sent one of their best members to encourage these new disciples. For the church in Jerusalem, this was a giant step forward.

There was no hesitation and no deliberation as to how the association with Gentiles might affect the image outsiders might have of the Jerusalem church. They had only one guiding question: "How can we help the church in Antioch?" Antioch represented new opportunities and potential for yielding unlimited growth.

Upon arrival, Barnabas was beside himself. Luke described his excitement: "Then when he [Barnabas] had come and witnessed the grace of God, he rejoiced and began to encourage them all with resolute heart to remain true to the Lord" (Acts 11:23).

A person's true spiritual stature can be evaluated by what causes that person great joy. Barnabas had no problem identifying God's providential hand at work in Antioch, and witnessing it thrilled his heart. It's the same feeling John expressed to Gaius when he wrote, "For I was very glad when brethren came and bore witness to your truth, that is, how you are walking in truth. I have no greater joy than this, to hear of my children walking in the truth" (3 John 3-4). Is it any wonder Barnabas received one of the most profound tributes made to any human being? Scripture testifies: "[F]or he [Barnabas] was a good man, and full of the Holy Spirit and of faith" (Acts 11:24).

It is interesting how Barnabas, a Levite (a member of a priestly tribe) and closely associated with Judaism, could suspend his Jewish connections to identify with Gentiles. Even Paul, whom Barnabas had brought to Antioch from Tarsus, began in this city to fulfill his divine mission of proclaiming the gospel to the Gentiles (Acts 9:15). Paul was as Jewish as they come – a "Hebrew of Hebrews" (Philippians 3:5). Do we possess such broad-mindedness as Barnabas and Paul? How often do our prejudicial inclinations hinder the progress of God's work?

Not only did the Jerusalem church have enough insight to see wonderful opportunities in Antioch, but the church in Antioch also saw rich opportunities in Jerusalem. As mentioned earlier, when the prophet Agabus was visiting Antioch, he informed the congregation a devastating famine was imminent. Instead of drawing up plans for their own survival, their minds turned toward their Jewish brothers and sisters in Judea: "And in the proportion that any of the disciples had means, each of them determined to send a contribution for the relief of the brethren living in Judea" (Acts 11:29).

The famine presented a perfect opportunity for Antioch to reciprocate a blessing. They had been blessed by those Jewish disciples who had brought the gospel to them, and now they could show their gratitude by coming to the aid of their Jewish brethren. This was an unparalleled gesture of unity. In fact, because Paul believed the positive ramifications of this contribution were of such a magnitude, he later encouraged Gentile congregations all over the Roman Empire to participate in similar opportunities (Acts 24:17; Romans 15:25-27; 1 Corinthians 16:1-2; 2 Corinthians 8 and 9). The Christians in Antioch were not governed by selfishness, but demonstrated a willing spirit of giving despite knowing they too could suffer severely from the famine which Agabus testified would touch everyone.

God's Family

The name Christian provided the foundation for both Jews and Gentiles to find a common basis for unity. According to John 19:19-20, the inscription attached to the cross above the head of the crucified Christ was "JESUS THE NAZARENE, THE KING OF THE JEWS." John informs us the inscription was written in three languages: Hebrew,

Latin and Greek; languages characterizing the vast diversity of cultures existing at the time of Jesus' death. The irony is that each of these three languages has contributed to the formation of the word "Christian." As H. Leo Boles noted:

> The *thought* is Jewish, denoting the Anointed One; the *root*, is Greek; the *termination*, *ianoi*, is Latin. So in the providence of God, the same three nations whose differing dialects proclaimed above the cross, "Jesus the King of the Jews," now unite in forming a word which for all time shall be applied to those who follow Christ (185).

"We're Christians!" is the motto of the followers of Christ. Christian is a glorious name. The name Christian defines who and what we really are. Christian is a sacred name. Wear it with honor. Wear it with dignity. Defend it with every ounce of strength. "The new name which here and now originated," wrote J.W. McGarvey in 1892, "proved the most potent name that has ever been applied to a body of men" (228).

Power Thoughts for Group Discussion

1. Find five instances in the Bible other than the ones mentioned in this chapter where people had their names changed by God. What was the reason behind each change?

2. How have prejudicial attitudes hindered the work of the church?

3. Should the church of today blend with the culture or should the church be counter-to-the-culture? What are the advantages and disadvantages of each approach?

4. What divided the church in Corinth? Read 1 Corinthians 1:10-13. How can the same thing divide churches today?

5. The word "Christian" is found only three times in the New Testament. Find and discuss the significance of each occurrence.

Chapter 13

The Courage to Pray

Acts 12:1-12

*"More things are wrought by prayer
than this world dreams of."*
Alfred Lord Tennyson

While preaching in a small town, I came across a political cartoon in the local newspaper. The setting of the cartoon was a school classroom where three young people sat at their desks. The first student had her hands over her eyes crying uncontrollably; the second student was staring in horror at an exam lying on his desk. He had a pencil in his mouth already broken in two by his vigorous gnawing. The third student had her hands clutched together while praying intently. Two teachers were pictured standing in the background observing the whole scene. The caption read, "No matter what the courts say, as long as there's testing, there will be prayers in school!"

The Threat of Prayer

For many years now, a calculated effort has been made to keep prayer out of public schools. Prayer, the opponents declare, is a clear violation of the separation between church and state. There is more to it, however, than this baseless accusation. The more secular our society becomes the more determined the forces of evil are in getting rid of prayer in every shape and form. Some people assert that praying is nothing but a superstition, an exercise for the non-intellectual. Prayer in the view of other people is considered a sign of the immaturity and insecurity of people who obviously cannot deal with life and its problems. That is what the pseudo-intellectual opponents are thinking.

If prayer is such a childish thing to do, as many say, one wonders why there is such a horde of militants protesting it. If it is a harmless exercise, leave us alone. Let us pray if we want. To be sure, the visual assaults against those who hold religious convictions pertaining to prayer are but small glimpses into the real spiritual battle being fought.

On one occasion the disciples came to Jesus and asked Him to teach them to pray (Luke 11:1). Do we need to learn how to pray, as Paul stated, "without ceasing" (1 Thessalonians 5:17)? After looking at the reasons why we should pray as seen in Acts 12:1-24, we will be motivated to devote more of our time to its development in our lives.

The Need Is Real

Before exploring some of the reasons why prayer is so important to our spiritual well being, maybe we should begin with an even more fundamental issue: Why should we bother to pray anyway? Is there really any need for us to pray? The answers to these questions are important, but let us first ask a few more questions to illustrate the kind of need we're talking about.

Do you honestly feel secure where you live and work? Do you feel safe? Is your life free from fear and anxiety? Do you not lock your doors at night? Why? Because it's not safe. The crime section in the local paper reported a string of burglaries in my neighborhood recently. I know personally how vulnerable we are. Perhaps you can relate to the shock of coming home from work, a trip or from visiting friends, only to discover your house in shambles, one of your cars stolen, or other precious items missing. To make matters worse, thieves no longer wait until no one is at home or for the cover of darkness. Crime happens now in broad daylight.

Do we not take precautions when we go shopping or even take a stroll around the block? Security guards are stationed everywhere today – in parking lots, at grocery stores, and even in some church buildings! Certainly, these facts alone illustrate how desperate the need is for us to pray.

• *Our Spiritual Nemesis.* Herod Agrippa (Acts 12:1) reigned over the land of Palestine in A.D. 42-44. He was the grandson of Herod the Great and the nephew of Herod Antipas, two very corrupt and cruel leaders. Herod the Great, in a fit of unbridled rage, ordered the slaughter of male children 2 years old and younger in an attempt to murder the infant child Jesus (Matthew 2:16). Herod Antipas' lust was aroused one day when the daughter of Herodias danced before him. Pleased by her provocative display, Herod promised her whatever she wanted. She requested the head of John the Baptist on a platter. Regrettably, Herod honored the request (14:1-12). Herod Agrippa was not the least disappointing of his relatives. He too was cut from the same mold. Only prayer can counter the spread of evil when a person like Herod Agrippa is in power. Paul warned about evil days ahead: "Therefore be careful how you walk, not as unwise men, but as wise, making the most of your time, because the days are evil" (Ephesians 5:15-16).

Evil stalks the land as Satan, our spiritual nemesis, roams about like a "roaring lion, seeking someone to devour" (1 Peter 5:8). Our most powerful defense is prayer. Only through prayer can we firmly resist him.

• *Prayer Helps the Pain.* Have you ever been falsely accused of anything? Have you ever been singled out because you were religious and ridiculed or treated unfairly? You wouldn't be alone if you answered "yes" to any of these questions. "[A]ll who desire to live godly in Christ Jesus," wrote Paul, "will be persecuted" (2 Timothy 3:12). Persecution presents the second reason why there's a need for you to pray.

King Herod "laid hands on some who belonged to the church, in order to mistreat them" (Acts 12:1). Nothing in the text indicates why he acted so cruelly. The actions of the church didn't warrant such merciless abuse by the authorities. Before this time, all persecutions suffered by the disciples of Christ had come primarily from the Jewish Council. This persecution, however, was the first assault upon the church by Gentiles.

Herod murdered the apostle James. Because the Jews were delighted with his actions, Herod arrested Peter and would have murdered him also if it had not been for the Jewish Passover.

The actions of Herod are shocking. But they really shouldn't be. After all, Jesus had warned His disciples, "Remember the word that I said to you, 'A slave is not greater than his master.' If they persecuted Me, they will also persecute you" (John 15:20). Notice what Jesus also said in the Beatitudes:

> Blessed are those who have been persecuted for the sake of righteousness, for theirs is the kingdom of heaven. Blessed are you when men cast insults at you, and persecute you, and say all kinds of evil against you falsely, on account of Me. Rejoice, and be glad, for your reward in heaven is great, for so they persecuted the prophets who were before you (Matthew 5:10-12).

Cruel and senseless persecutions present a real need for the people of God to pray.

• *Time Is Running Out.* A third reason why there's a need to pray is found in the urgency created by the elapse of time. Again, a few questions will illustrate the point. Do you ever feel that time is slipping away? Have you ever wished you could turn back the hands on the clock? Meeting a deadline, waiting for an approaching doctor's visit, or pacing in a surgical waiting room while a loved one undergoes surgery are all demanding circumstances. These intense periods of time generate frustration, fear and fatigue. This is precisely why in these types of situations many sense a strong urgency to pray.

Herod seized Peter and threw him in prison, and four squads of soldiers guarded Peter. Only a few days remained until Peter would be carried away to execution. Time was of the utmost importance. What was the church going to do? Luke wrote: "So Peter was kept in the prison, but prayer for him was being made fervently by the church to God" (Acts 12:5).

Peter's predicament appeared hopeless; yet, very subtly, Luke indicates by the words "but prayer" why the story isn't over yet. It has been said prayers and tears are the church's arms; therewith she fights, not only against her enemies, but also for her friends. The church knew time was running out, so members appealed to the One who is timeless. Paul wanted Timothy to understand the importance of prayer when he wrote:

First of all, then, I urge that entreaties and prayers, petitions and thanksgivings, be made on behalf of all men, for kings and all who are in authority, in order that we may lead a tranquil and quiet life in all godliness and dignity. This is good and acceptable in the sight of God our Savior, who desires all men to be saved and to come to the knowledge of the truth (1 Timothy 2:1-4).

As long as the clock keeps ticking, and evil continues to prey upon the disciples of Christ, there will always be good reasons for devoting more time to prayer.

Pray Without Ceasing

Because we have seen the need to pray, let's explore why we should pray without ceasing.

• *A Sympathetic Ear.* First, prayer is our personal link to God. Millions of people long for others to listen to them – to their problems, their struggles and their frustrations. Recently, someone visited me in my office. I could tell she only wanted a sympathetic ear. As she was leaving, she thanked me and said I had helped her. Actually, I didn't say much at all. The act of listening was more important than anything else I could have said or done. Maybe Peter's mind was reflecting on his prison experience when he wrote, "For the eyes of the Lord are upon the righteous, And His ears attend to their prayer, But the face of the Lord is against those who do evil" (1 Peter 3:12). Christians can always find comfort in knowing they serve a God who extends to them a sympathetic ear: "Let us therefore draw near with confidence to the throne of grace, that we may receive mercy and may find grace to help in time of need" (Hebrews 4:16).

Matthew Henry said, "Wherever the people of God are they have a way open heavenward" (1682). How very true these words are!

• *What Prayer Can Do.* Second, we should pray because God acts on our behalf when we pray. If we took the time to look in retrospect, we would be amazed to see how God has answered many of our prayers in a powerful way. We may not have received exactly what we prayed for, but we would have to admit that what we actually got was better.

Look at how God responded to the church's prayer on behalf of Peter:

> And behold, an angel of the Lord suddenly appeared, and a light shone in the cell; and he struck Peter's side and roused him, saying, "Get up quickly." And his chains fell off his hands. And the angel said to him, "Gird yourself and put on your sandals." And he did so. And he said to him, "Wrap your cloak around you and follow me." And he went out and continued to follow, and he did not know that what was being done by the angel was real, but thought he was seeing a vision. And when they had passed the first and second guard, they came to the iron gate that leads into the city, which opened for them by itself; and they went out and went along one street; and immediately the angel departed from him. And when Peter came to himself, he said, "Now I know for sure that the Lord has sent forth His angel and rescued me from the hand of Herod and from all that the Jewish people were expecting" (Acts 12:7-11).

From a human perspective, Peter's predicament looked hopeless, but when God got involved, hopelessness was transformed into confident expectation. "When we rely upon organization," wrote A.C. Dixon, "we get what organization can do; when we rely upon education, we get what education can do; when we rely upon eloquence, we get what eloquence can do. ... But when we rely upon prayer, we get what God can do" (Glover 186). The movements of God should be enough to convince every Christian in the powerful potential of prayer.

The Benefits of Prayer

The benefits of prayer are really too numerous to list. However, there are three extremely important benefits that we should know about.

• *Deliverance.* One major way we benefit from prayer is experiencing the deliverance it brings. Have you ever been impressed as to how quickly and smoothly delicate problems seem to work themselves out? Maybe it was a problem with your boss, a certain employee, your spouse or a difficult child. Many church leaders wrestle with finding solutions to delicate problems; yet, somehow by God's providence, these problems are resolved.

Acts 12:13-17 is somewhat comical. Note how the church reacted when Peter knocked on the door. Rhoda was so excited about hearing Peter's voice she forgot to open the door to let him in. When Rhoda told the others Peter was at the door, they doubted her words. Finally, after the door was opened, they were amazed to see Peter standing there. Why were they so shocked? Had they not been fervently praying for his release from prison? Was it because God had responded so quickly to their request? The fact is God answered their prayer and that same God will answer our prayers.

• *Encouragement.* In addition to the deliverance prayer can bring, prayer is an attitude lifter. God encourages us through prayer. Surely there have been times when our faith has been strengthened because we knew that God answered our prayers. It is encouraging to hear fellow Christians share their stories about how God has worked in their lives. Likewise, when those who had gathered saw Peter, they were encouraged. Joy filled Rhoda's heart. Excitement emanated from the others to such a degree that Peter had to motion for them to keep quiet. Peter said to them, "Report these things to James and the brethren" (Acts 12:17). The church throughout Jerusalem would be encouraged and strengthened by such news. Likewise, we encourage our brothers and sisters in Christ when we pray for them.

• *Vindication.* The most interesting benefit of prayer is the ultimate vindication we enjoy by trusting in its power. Why should we be honest, fair and dependable, when people around us are not? Why put forth the effort? The wicked seem to prosper, and we who want to do right appear to be at a disadvantage. It is not fair! If that describes you, you're not feeling anything that other Christians haven't felt before.

Herod executed the guards who kept watch over Peter. He left Jerusalem and carried his anger with him to Caesarea. Luke tells us Herod became very hostile toward the people of Tyre and Sidon. We are not told the reason why, but it is clear the people of Tyre and Sidon wanted to be on Herod's good side. After many entreaties, Herod finally granted them a hearing:

> And on an appointed day Herod, having put on his royal apparel, took his seat on the rostrum and began delivering an

address to them. And the people kept crying out, "The voice of a god and not of a man!" And immediately an angel of the Lord struck him because he did not give God the glory, and he was eaten by worms and died (Acts 12:21-23).

Josephus, a Jewish historian of the first century, also described what happened to Herod. He said a sudden pain gripped Herod's bowels and five days later he died (*Antiquities*, XIX, VIII, 2). No matter how bleak things may appear, the righteous will be exalted and the wicked will be overthrown. People of truth will ultimately be vindicated.

Our Greatest Weapon

Because there is such an urgent need to pray, a tremendous potential in prayer, and obviously wonderful benefits received from prayer, then one question remains: Why aren't we spending more time in prayer?

Frank Peretti's book, *This Present Darkness*, is a fictional novel about the spiritual battle in which we as Christians are engaged. With imagination he describes the spiritual world where the battle between right and wrong really occurs. His book is actually a story about the power of prayer. Evil spirits invaded a small town and made a concentrated effort to overtake it. The demon world dominated the thoughts and the actions of most of the people living there. With the help of a small-town church and a courageous preacher, the forces of evil were destroyed. Prayer was the weapon that defeated the darkness. The angels of God were energized by prayer, and the longer and harder and more determined the little congregation prayed, the stronger and bigger and more powerful the angels of God became. When fully energized by prayer, the angels were able to crush the evil demons. Sadly, the angels almost lost the battle because there were not enough people praying.

God's people must pray. There's no telling what can happen when God gets involved! Is God involved in your life? Have you prayed lately? Do you now have the courage to pray?

Power Thoughts for Group Discussion

1. What situations in your life have moved you to go to God in prayer? What were the results?

2. Why should Christians not be reluctant to share with others how God has been working in their lives?

3. Paul wrote, "And we know that God causes all things to work together for good to those who love God, to those who are called according to His purpose" (Romans 8:28). What does this verse teach about God's work in our lives and world?

4. In the current debate over the separation of church and state, why is the issue of prayer so prominent?

5. Make a list of what can be learned about the value of prayer from the example of Daniel as recorded in Daniel 6:1-24.

Afterword

We have studied together 13 ways the church of the first century found the courage to stay the course. Each chapter revealed a pivotal period in the life of the early Christians. The manner in which they confronted the challenges they faced is more than inspirational, it's compelling.

The church today is at a crossroad; it's our time to step forward, following the example of our brothers and sisters of long ago. God's Word is just as powerful as it was then; God's promises are just as sure, and His presence is just as real! The church of our Lord Jesus Christ cannot sit idly on the sidelines, nor can she fade into the background, conforming to the world instead of transforming it. The restoration of biblical Christianity still remains the most ambitious challenge ever to face the church today.

But the restoration of biblical Christianity means more than the restoration of biblical doctrines such as the plan of salvation, the organization of the church, and the kind of worship pleasing to God. Doctrine without the right spirit is just as debilitating as the right spirit without doctrine – both are meaningless, empty and worthless. We seek to worship God in spirit and truth (John 4:24).

Sept. 11, 2001, was a pivotal event in our nation's history. We learned about ourselves on that day; we reflected upon the meaning of our existence, and we became aware of how vulnerable we really are.

What is the present status of the Lord's church? Have her members become discouraged, disenchanted or disillusioned? The church will always face battles within her fellowship and battles from without. How she faces them is the critical issue. Will we have the courage to eliminate our prejudices, pride and personal agendas as we seek unity, forgiveness and personal holiness? Will we have the courage to follow Jesus in serving and loving others? Will we have the courage to defend the truth of God in a spirit of gentleness against the encroachment of doctrinal errors and world philosophies?

It takes just as much courage today to be a Christian as it did in the book of Acts. However, there is not a challenge facing us that cannot be met head-on when we capture the courage of our brothers and sisters in the first century.

Works Cited

Barclay, William. *The Acts of the Apostles*. Rev. ed. Philadelphia: Westminster Press, 1976.

Bartlett, John. *Familiar Quotations*. Boston: Little, Brown and Co., Rev. 1992.

Boles, H. Leo. *A Commentary on Acts of the Apostles*. Nashville: Gospel Advocate, 1989.

Bruce, F.F. *The Book of the Acts*. Rev. ed. Grand Rapids: Eerdman's, 1988.

Cheney, Lois A. *God Is No Fool*. Nashville: Abingdon Press, 1969.

Dyrness, William A. *How Does America Hear the Gospel*. Grand Rapids: Eerdman's, 1989.

Eusebius, Pamphilus. *Ecclesiastical History*. Grand Rapids: Baker Book House, 1989, reprint.

Glover, Robert. *Bible Basis of Missions*. Bible House of Los Angeles, 1946.

Henry, Matthew. *Commentary on the Whole Bible*. Grand Rapids: Eerdman's, 1961.

Josephus, Flavius. *Antiquities of the Jews*. Trans. William Whiston. Grand Rapids: Baker Book House, 1979, reprint.

Talbott, Strobe. "Defiance." *Time* Magazine 19 June 1989: 9.

McGarvey, J.W. *New Commentary on Acts of the Apostles*. Cincinnati: Standard Publishing, 1892.

McGinnis, Alan Loy. *The Friendship Factor*. Minneapolis: Augsburg Publishing House, 1979.

McIntosh, Gary and Glen Martin. *Finding them, Keeping Them*. Nashville: Broadman Press, 1992.

Morison, Frank. *Who Moved the Stone*. Grand Rapids: Zondervan, 1987.

Wiersbe, Warren. *Be Dynamic*. Wheaton: Victor Books, 1989.

Young, Robert. *Young's Analytical Concordance to the Bible*. Peabody, Mass.: Hendrickson Publishers, 1984.

About the Author

Dr. G. Scott Gleaves is the minister of the Timberlane Church of Christ in Tallahassee, Fla. He has also served congregations in Texas, Tennessee, and Alabama.

Scott received his bachelor's degree from Lipscomb University in Nashville, Tenn.; two master's degrees from Abilene Christian University in Abilene, Texas; and a doctorate from Southern Christian University in Montgomery, Ala. Scott is married to the former Sherri Boddy and has three children – Lindsay, Nathan and Taylor.

Scott's articles have appeared in the *Gospel Advocate*, *Christian Bible Teacher*, and the *Restoration Quarterly*. He has also written a book, *For Theirs Is the Kingdom of God: Living by the Beatitudes*, which was published in 1997. Scott writes daily inspiration e-mails called *Power Thoughts*. For a free subscription, contact the Timberlane Church of Christ website, www.timberlane-coc.org.

meditation
John 5:39, 10:10

Printed in the United States
20118LVS00001B/385-453

9 780892 255375